D0065895

THE CONTEXT OF DECISION

GORDON D. KAUFMAN

the
CONTEXT of
DECISION
A THEOLOGICAL ANALYSIS

ABINGDON PRESS «» NEW YORK • NASHVILLE

THE CONTEXT OF DECISION

Copyright © 1961 by Abingdon Press

Library of Congress Catalog Card Number: 61-8410

SET UP, PRINTED, AND BOUND BY THE
PARTHENON PRESS, AT NASHVILLE,
TENNESSEE, UNITED STATES OF AMERICA

In gratitude for
die Stillen im Lande

PREFACE

⇌ This brief sketch of the theological foundations of the
Christian ethic was prepared on the invitation of Bethel
College (Kansas) to give the annual Menno Simons Lectures in 1959. The present text contains those lectures
somewhat revised.

The Menno Simons Lectureship was established "to pro-
mote research and public lectures . . . relating to Anabaptist-Mennonite history and development, theology and
practice, life and culture, or related subjects, both past
and present." The Anabaptist-Mennonite tradition has always emphasized the centrality of God's love in his revelation of himself in Jesus Christ, together with the requisite
centrality of love for both neighbor and enemy in the life
of the acting Christian. Accordingly, in other series of the

7

Menno Simons Lectures historical reports on the ways in which these emphases have been developed in Anabaptist-Mennonite history as well as the ways in which they were understood by the biblical writers themselves, have been set forth. In this series of lectures, however, I have been concerned with a closely related though distinct theme, namely an investigation of the meaning of these emphases for twentieth-century man.

It is sometimes thought that the Christian ethic, in contrast with philosophical ethics, is concerned largely with systematic formulation of moral precepts and attitudes derived from tradition, particularly the Bible. Certainly it is true that in the Christian church thinking is carried on in conscious awareness of the community of believers, living and dead, which is its context, and the dependence of contemporary thinkers on the traditions in which the earlier struggles of Christians are handed on to us is unquestionable.

Nevertheless, it is never possible for us simply to take over the traditions which have been handed down to us, whether these be Mennonite or Presbyterian, Protestant or Catholic, for we live in a world very different in many respects from our predecessors. This is true not only with respect to our environment of artifacts such as automobiles, electrical appliances, printed books, newspapers, and the like. Far more important, our very ways of thought are radically different from those, for example, of the Reformation period, to say nothing of the first-century Christians. Those men knew nothing of a scientific world view in which the earth revolves around the sun instead of vice versa; they lived for the most part in a three-story universe with heaven above, hell beneath, and the world of man in between. They had no opportunity to participate in forms of social organization, such as we have in contemporary democracy, in which even small minorities can take some active and responsible part in government. Their socio-economic life had not been transformed by modern industrialization and banking into a vast network of interdependent structures which very literally makes it impossible for the Christian to live separated in any *essential* way from the fundamentally secular life of the nation-state in which he resides. Nor did they—despite important anticipations in this regard in the Christian understanding of man's sinfulness—have any clear awareness of the way in which the conscious processes of human thought and action are influenced by sociological and psychological factors, as Marx and Freud and their disciples have taught us.

In short, the kind of socio-cultural world in which the men of the Reformation (and certainly the first-century Christians) lived was so very different from our own that it is impossible for us simply to take over unaltered the great traditions which they have passed on to us. It is just as essential for Christian as for philosophical ethics to think through afresh the problems of decision and purpose and value in terms of the new situation faced by each generation. Systematic Christian ethics is concerned with just this unavoidable task.

Moreover, even were it possible to avoid the task, doing so would be a refusal to, as Paul says, "work out [our] own salvation with fear and trembling" (Phil. 2:12). Instead of ourselves bearing full responsibility before God for our attitudes, ideas, and beliefs, we would be seeking to shift responsibility to earlier generations. We must, then—if we are serious about being Christians in the twentieth century —attempt to think through for our own generation, our own world, and ourselves, the meaning of love for neighbor and

enemy in response to God's love for us. No one can absolve us from this responsibility or perform this task for us.
To refuse it is to refuse the specific work God has given
this generation, the task of being Christians in the twentieth
century. Systematic Christian ethics is concerned with just
this unavoidable obligation.

In a work as brief as the present one it is not possible
to survey the whole gamut of personal and social problems
which should be analyzed in a fully developed Christian
ethic. The ingredient common to all such problems, however—that which makes them precisely *moral* problems—is
the imperative they lay upon us to *decide and act* with
reference to them. They impinge on us in terms of values
to be realized, obligations to be fulfilled, and we find ourselves required to make some choice with reference to them.
Thus, central to ethics is the problem of decision, an issue
faced by every individual and group implicitly in each
moment and often explicitly. The present work is focused
on this problem which underlies every other moral question. I have sought here to clarify the problem of decision
as understood from within the perspective of Christian
ethics.

After a brief introductory chapter which distinguishes
Christian ethics from humanistic ethics on the one side and
naturalistic ethics on the other, the analysis proceeds through
four steps. These can be visualized as concentric circles of
decreasing radius coming finally to a focus in the center
point which is the present moment of decision. Beginning
with the widest, each circle provides the context within
which the succeeding circles must be understood. Thus, we
begin (Chapter II) by seeking to define theologically the
metaphysical context within which decision occurs, viz.,

the relationship between man and the ultimate reality with which he has to do, God as made known in Jesus Christ. We proceed then (Chapter III) to the somewhat narrower *sociological context* of decision analyzed in terms of the problem of church and world. The analysis of each of these wider circles is presupposed as we turn (Chapter IV) to the *personal-biographical context* and seek to uncover theologically the Christian understanding of the free and creative individual. Thus, finally (Chapter V), it becomes possible to analyze the moment of choice itself, paying particular attention to the problem of guides or criteria of right decision. (The analysis here utilizes as a critical specimen the problem of the Christian's attitude toward national defense and war.)

Thanks are due to many who have directly or indirectly assisted in the writing of this book. First, to my Mennonite heritage which provided me with a keen awareness of the ethical dimension of the Christian faith through its emphasizing Christian nonresistance. Second, to my teacher of Christian ethics, H. Richard Niebuhr of Yale, who first taught me to think theologically about the problem of decision, and to whom I am indebted for much set forth herein without explicit acknowledgment. Third, to my wife and children who have helped me to realize more fully what personal existence actually is, as well as how difficult are its problems. Fourth, to my students at Pomona College and Vanderbilt Divinity School who were the first ones exposed to some of these ideas, and whose criticism helped sharpen the issues. Fifth, to Bethel College for providing the occasion to sketch out this understanding of the Christian ethic by the kind invitation to give the Menno Simons Lectures in 1959. Finally, to my colleague, James

Sellers, professor of Christian ethics at Vanderbilt, and my former colleague, Everett Tilson, each of whom carefully and critically read this manuscript in an early stage of its development.

GORDON D. KAUFMAN

CONTENTS

1 The Nature of Christian Ethics

"In this is love, not that we loved God but that he loved us and sent his Son to be the expiation for our sins. Beloved, if God so loved us, we also ought to love one another. No man has ever seen God; if we love one another, God abides in us and his love is perfected in us. . . . God is love, and he who abides in love abides in God, and God abides in him."
(I John 4:10-12, 16*b*)

CHRISTIAN ETHICS IS THE ATTEMPT TO DEFINE AND understand, from a Christian point of view, what it means to be a deciding, purposing, and acting self in the midst of various communities (both Christian and non-Christian) of similar selves. In more familiar words, it is the attempt to delineate, understand, and interpret the Christian life.

Three things must be said immediately by way of clarification. First, Christian ethics is a part of theology. Christian theology is the attempt (which must be carried through in every generation) to understand and interpret God, man, the world, and their interrelation, from the point of view of Christian faith. For this purpose theology develops such massive interpretive concepts as the doctrines of creation, sin, atonement, providence, last things, and so forth, each of which must be understood afresh as each generation apprehends anew its own existence-in-the-world-at-the-hands-of-God. Christian ethics, now, is concerned with those elements of our experience and situation which arise from the fact that we are *living* beings, continuously called upon to *decide* and *act*. Inasmuch, however, as these dimensions cannot be understood in abstraction from the totality of our existence, it is clear that Christian ethics is a part of the larger whole which is theology. Therefore, it will be necessary in these chapters for us to deal with certain fundamental theological doctrines in order to grasp the peculiar character of the Christian ethic.

The second thing to be said by way of general clarification is that Christian ethics is not concerned simply with the interpretation of the life of Christians. In the first place, Christians are in constant commerce with non-Christians, so it would not be possible to interpret Christian decisions and acts without dealing simultaneously with non-Christian ones. In the second place, the Christian gospel has to do with God's relation to the *world* (not simply to the church or to Christians), and Christian theology, therefore, must seek to understand and interpret the life and decisions of *all* men before God, however important be the distinction between Christian and non-Christian. It would be the highest form of spiritual pride, combined with a radical lack of faith in God's redemptive power amongst those we find difficult to recognize as Christian, to say that the "Christian life" with which Christian ethics is concerned is simply *our* life. Christian ethics, then, must attempt to understand and interpret the problems of deciding and acting both of Christian and non-Christian, church and world—but always from a Christian point of view.

My third general remark is this: Christian ethics will not give us the *answers* to our moral problems; it will not give us the *right decisions* on specific questions which we face. Christian ethics seeks to discern norms which can be guides and aids in making decisions, and it relates, unifies, and organizes these within the context of Christian theology, removing contradictions and inconsistencies. It can thus deepen moral sensitivity and increase awareness of the wider implications of our actions. But in the concrete situations in which we are called upon to act, *we ourselves* must finally make the decision as to what we should do, and we alone bear the responsibility for that decision. The study of ethics throws light on my responsibilities as a father in a family, as well as my obligations to starving children in India, but it cannot absolve me from the task of finally deciding myself whether I should give more time and money to the next relief drive and proportionately less to my children. How and when various principles and norms developed in Christian ethics apply to the actual world of decisions and actions and persons in which we live, we determine in the moment we make a choice and set ourselves to the realization of a purpose. It is thus an error to suppose that Christian ethics can tell us how to act in every, or indeed any, concrete situation. However much reflective study aids our discerning the wide ramifications of love, the actual responsibility before God for any decisions we make remains always our own. It is for this reason that, as Paul says, it is with "fear and trembling" that we must "work out [our] own salvation" knowing that "God is at work in [us], both to will and to work for his good pleasure" (Phil. 2:12-13).

Our principal concern in these chapters will be to gain

some understanding of the problems of decision and action from a Christian point of view.

I

Where, now, do we begin? What is a proper starting-point for sketching out the structure of the Christian ethic? What is the basis on which Christian ethics rests? There are two quite distinct ways which might be followed in trying to answer these questions. They may be designated as the *dogmatic* way and the *comparative-analytic* way.

We utilize a dogmatic method when our answer to these questions is given simply by reference to a *dogma* which we take to be obviously true. For example, we may say that Christian ethics rests in the main on rules of conduct found in the Bible; or Christian ethics is the practical application of the teachings of the church; or Christian ethics has its foundation in the deliverances of the individual conscience. Each of these is dogmatic in that it begins with a dogma and then proceeds to sketch out the Christian ethic through unfolding the implications of the dogma.

The comparative-analytic method proceeds in somewhat different fashion. Here we are concerned to uncover and analyze the overall Christian perspective, as it has expressed itself in the history of the Christian community, through comparison with other significant perspectives which, by their contrast, throw light on what is distinctively Christian. The comparative-analytic method has the advantage of not requiring prior acceptance of a particular dogma before one can proceed. Moreover, it facilitates placing the variety of dogmatic claims in their proper positions within the Christian viewpoint. But precisely because it is thus some-what broader and more general it does not lend itself to reaching quick conclusions on concrete and specific issues. We shall begin with a comparative-analytic procedure.

Ethics, we have said, is concerned with the analysis of decision and action. Now it ought to be clear at the outset that all action involves the interrelation of two factors, the *actor* and the *situation* in which he acts. What right action is will depend both on the nature of that which acts and on the nature of the situation in which the acting is going on. Every ethic, therefore, in attempting to uncover the nature of right action will involve an understanding of: a) man, the actor; b) the context within which action occurs; and c) the relationship between them. The answer to the question of right and wrong will depend in many respects on the interpretation of these three items. Hence, if we can see the distinctiveness of the Christian understanding of them, we will be well on the way to grasping the characteristic perspective of Christian ethics.

There is not time to make detailed comparisons of a wide variety of points of view. We can briefly examine three types of perspectives, however, and thus make clear the crucial point. Before proceeding it should be noted that no attempt will be made here to consider all of the ramifications of each point of view outlined. Nor will I seek to do full justice to the significance or meaning of each position. Our concern with these several "ideal types" of ethico-metaphysical viewpoints will be simply and solely to sharpen our awareness of the *distinctive* character of the Christian perspective on reality and the place of human decision and action within it. It may well be, therefore, that no actual historical representative of, e.g., "humanism" or "naturalism" corresponds exactly to what I am designating by these terms, and that frequently, or perhaps always, a mixture of two or more of these types is found in actual historical figures. But if what is said about these view-points appears to be inadequate or one-sided, this is not due to a desire to be invidious. Rather, it is because we are concerned with these positions only for the purpose of getting our bearings for a closer and more detailed look at the peculiar perspective of the Christian ethic.

Consider then, for example, how the moral problem is shaped by a point of view that holds there is *no morally significant relationship between man and his cosmic environment*. This is not an uncommon position. Man is often held to be merely a chance product of the evolutionary process, evolution itself being thought of as a blind movement with no purposive will giving it direction and character. On this view, whatever forms of life evolve are simply there, and they must survive as best they can. Man is on his own in this world; what becomes of him does not depend on any God who has placed him here. It depends on one thing alone: whether he is able to adapt himself successfully to his natural environment. It is not difficult to see the kind of ethics that is consonant with this general perspective. Whatever enables man to stay alive and get as much as he can out of life is regarded as right. The only meaningful restrictions on his behavior grow out of the requirements for his survival and happiness. Man can (and should) utilize and even exploit nature and other creatures. The cosmology which views man as fundamentally an accident produced by the natural process results, thus, in an *anthropocentric* ethic, right being defined in terms of human need and desire. It is to this point of view that the name *humanism* may appropriately be applied.

There are several kinds of humanistic ethics, varying according to their views of the nature of man. For example, man may be regarded as fundamentally a social creature with human friendship and community understood as among the great goods of life. Here a two-sided ethic generally develops. On the one hand, it is held that one's relations to his fellows should be governed by altruistic ideals such as service to the neighbor and to all men. On the other hand, it is regarded as right and proper that men should co-operate in science and technology to exploit nature for man's benefit; natural resources should be carefully used to build a high culture and civilization. For this as for every form of humanism, man is not responsible to nature or to God for what he does; men are responsible only to each other and to future generations. Often such an anthropocentric ethic has lofty ideals, and those committed to it may lead devoted lives of real service to humanity. But it must also be observed that potentially demonic orientations, such as various nationalisms and ethnocentrisms, as well as Marxian communism, are expressions of this type of social humanism.

A quite different type of humanistic ethic results if man is understood in primarily individualistic terms. Here humanism becomes egoistic hedonism. Every man is on his own; hence, each should strive to get as much from life, and to give as little, as possible. A familiar expression of this self-centered form of humanism is the laissez-faire economic ethic of capitalism with its demand that each should seek to maximize his profit. Sometimes this individualistic humanism takes more "idealistic" forms. For example, an artist may claim the right to develop his own aesthetic interest and talents without regard to their effects on other human beings; or a scientist may devote himself to his interest in "truth" whether this be beneficial for humanity at large or not; in America it is thought to be almost beyond question that every man has the right to pursue his own happiness.

It is not necessary to go into further detail on the various forms of humanism, social or individualistic. The central point with which we are concerned ought to be clear, namely, that humanism is a distinctive and important kind of ethic which is closely correlated with a definite conception of the relation—or better, absence of significant relation—between man and the cosmic environment in which he finds himself. No doubt all of us in our ethical thinking and action often proceed on humanistic assumptions, perhaps in our economic or political life, perhaps in our pursuit of the values of social and cultural life, perhaps in other contexts. Later, we shall look more explicitly at the relationship between humanism and the Christian perspective.

II

Let us turn now to a second kind of cosmological orientation and see how it expresses itself in an ethic. Suppose that one believes the universe has not developed simply by chance (a view which probably no one holds in its extreme form), but that it has a rational structure of some sort. On this view everything that happens has its reason and cause, and much if not everything about nature might well be comprehensible to human reason. Thus, the evolutionary process was not a series of accidents for which no account can be be given; on the contrary, every stage of that process was an inevitable development out of previous stages according to the laws of nature, and the whole process is in principle (if not in fact) comprehensible to scientific man studying nature and gradually uncovering her laws. Here in sharp contrast with the previous view, man, along with every other being

in nature, has a definite place in the total process which is
his *proper* place. He is not free to choose any pattern of life
he desires. He must fit himself into Nature in accordance
with her structure. Since this is the basic reality with which
man has to do, right and wrong must be defined in terms
of man's proper playing of the role Nature has given him.

The ethic that grows out of this point of view is not
primarily humanistic; it is *naturalistic*. Here many restrictions
are laid on man from without. The good life is not simply
the realization of human needs and desires, as in humanism;
it is primarily conceived in terms of man's submission to
Nature and her laws. The problem of ethics is, on the one
hand, discerning man's place in the world, and, on the other
hand, seeking adequately to fit into that place. The resources of science and philosophy, the methods of mystical
intuition, the disciplines of meditation and submission, may
separately or in some combination be advocated as the proper
solution to the ethical problem. But always the ethic that
flows from naturalism (as here conceived) is primarily an
ethic of submission to the order of Nature.

For this perspective, the question of whether man is fundamentally individual or social is not as important as for
humanism; this is simply a part of the larger question of the
Nature into which we must fit ourselves. The more important question for naturalism has to do with the method of
discovering our proper place. For ancient stoicism—the
classical form of what I have been calling naturalism—it is
through reason that man comes to a proper understanding of
his true role. In more modern naturalists scientific investigation supposedly discovers to us the answer to this question.
But there are other views also. Romanticism, for example,
holds that through feeling we find our proper place in the
world. And in this it is related both to mysticism, with its

longing for the feeling of oneness with all Reality, and to contemporary existentialism. Again, voluntaristic forms of naturalism, rooted in a conception of the cosmos as dynamic, insist that only in creative action, perhaps in accordance with the direction of cosmic evolution, is the proper role for man found. However diverse are these various points of view, all are naturalistic in the sense here defined: they all understand the good life in terms of man's finding his proper place in the world.

III

I would like to sketch a third world view, similar in some respects to those just mentioned, yet radically different. This view is like naturalism in that it sees that man's life must be understood in terms of the context in which it falls—however, here the context is not nature, but history. That is, the world is understood fundamentally, not as natural process following fixed laws of nature, but as historical struggle between competing personal wills. It is a world continuously being created into something new and different. Here nature is not apprehended simply as the impersonal context in which personal lives appear; rather, she is the deliberate expression of creative will. In its emphasis on the personal and historical as the key to what is of real importance, this view resembles humanism; but in the insistence that man's life must be understood in terms of its context and must be conformed and submitted to the demands of that context, it resembles naturalism. We can appropriately call this point of view *historicism*, since history is the form of the reality with which man here has to do.

The most common example of what I am here calling historicism, and the one with which we are principally concerned, is the perspective of the biblical writers. (Hegel, Marx, Nietzsche, Heidegger and others in varying degrees and ways represent this viewpoint in nontheistic forms.) For the biblical writers the world process, nature, is the product of the creative and purposive will of God. It is God who brought this world into being, and through it he is carrying out his own purposes, acting on it, changing it, transforming it in various ways. Man's proper role in life is here assigned him by God; human life finds its true meaning so far as it is a fulfillment of the purposes of God. But since God is conceived as living and personal—and not as the impersonal structure of nature, as in naturalism—it is not possible to define laws of conduct or right action (corresponding to laws of nature) which hold once and for all. Rather, right action here will simply be living-as-a-person-in-community with God, on the one hand, and one's fellow men, on the other. To live in community, it should be evident, involves much more than merely following out some pattern of absolute values or ideals or laws which have once for all been laid down as norms of conduct. To live in community is to live in *responsiveness* to the other persons in the community, to listen when they speak and to answer honestly and relevantly and significantly, to minister to their needs and to allow them to minister to yours. In short, it is to be a living and responsive *thou* to their *I's*.

From this point of view the task of ethics is not the isolating of some ultimate standard of right and wrong, then insisting on conformity to that standard. Rather, the concern here is to be responsive to the voice of the living God as he confronts and speaks to us in every moment, to live as human persons before this supreme Person, that is, to act creatively and freely in every moment in response to his will for that moment. In short, it is to enter into community with God and his other creatures, or, to use the biblical symbol, it is to participate in the kingdom of God. All of humanism's awareness of man's uniqueness and difference from nature, of man's creativity and freedom, is taken up into this view, but this is not humanism. All of naturalism's awareness, that man must submit to that which is greater than he and of which he is a mere product, is also taken up into this view, but this is not naturalism. Though each of these other views has its own way of dealing with man's historicity, the historicism of the Christian faith is a unique orientation through which man's place in the world, and the good life for man, come to have a quite extraordinary meaning. The remainder of this book will be devoted to an exploration of this meaning.

IV

Though certain marks of the Christian point of view have become clear through discussing it as historicism in contrast with naturalism and humanism, we have not yet uncovered its full distinctiveness. For the Bible not only makes the claim that the form of man's relations to the ultimately real is personal-historical; it also proceeds to fill out in some detail the actual turn that history has taken and the concrete character those personal relations have come to possess. And the picture which it paints here is a very odd, not to say terrifying, one. For along with its claim that community with God and fellows is the true context—indeed the very source and basis—of human existence, we find the disclosure that precisely this community has become disrupted and distorted to the point of near destruction. It is an unhappy history that is reported in the Bible. The personal relations between God's children and God, instead of being characterized by love and responsiveness can be more aptly described in terms of estrangement, distrust, disloyalty, and guilt. Man has become alienated from God and from fellow man. The very community in and through which man was to find his true being has moved through a history which has disrupted it and which accordingly stunts and corrupts all men who emerge within it. Men are no longer whole and healthy; they are sick and weak. Men no longer live in vital and sound relationship with that Reality which is the source and ground of their being; they live in a world of illusion and delusion, confused and out of touch with their True Good.

We must save for later chapters our analysis of the full meaning and significance of this view and the warrant for it. But we must note here its revolutionary implications for the task of ethics. If man actually is not in rapport with God—that is, with the ultimately real—if man's whole being is in fact somehow distorted, then it will not be possible for him by his own efforts to come to true understanding of himself and his problems, nor can he resolve his difficulties. The presupposition of every non-Christian ethical analysis is that in some way, by some method, through some kind of intuition or insight, man can come to know the good and the right and can do them. Naturalism assumes that we can know nature and our own place in it; non-Christian forms of historicism claim that we can discover the meaning of history and our historicity and thus find our true role; humanism supposes we can understand our own deepest needs and desires. Each assumes that man is fundamentally in rapport with whatever reality it is necessary to know in order to apprehend and do the right.

But if this assumption is false, then ethics is radically transformed. If men are actually estranged from Reality—

whether conceived as self, nature, history, or God—they will be unable to achieve a true or precise analysis of themselves or their situation, and they will not come to know the right, however persistently they might suppose themselves to be pursuing it. Moreover, if their very selves are stunted and distorted, even were they able to gain such true knowledge, their deceitful feelings and disobedient wills would make it impossible to actualize this knowledge in their lives. In short, the human situation would be a tragic trap from which no escape were possible. What sense, from this point of view, could ethical inquiry possibly have?

But the Christian point of view is not, after all, simply a description of the human situation as hopeless; it is fundamentally a *gospel*, a proclamation of *good news*. And the good news is precisely this: that God—that One from whom man is so tragically estranged—has acted and does act to rescue man from his hopeless plight. From the human point of view there is no possibility of escape. Man is caught in quicksand and every struggle only mires him deeper. But God has acted from beyond this human situation, this quicksand, to pull man out and give him new life. Hence, in and through this action man comes into a new rapport with the Real; now he can come to know the good, to take pleasure in it, to desire it, and to do it.

Now if this Christian view of man's situation is correct and man's relation to God is characterized not only by estrangement but also by God's redemption, then ethics becomes something new and different. Clearly, ethical analysis cannot begin with or be based upon human insights, ideas, or attitudes, for all of these are distorted; rather, it must have its basis in and through what happens in God's act. His act of revelation of his will becomes the source of such knowledge of the good as we come to possess; his act of redemption of our wills enables such doing of the good as becomes possible for us. Christian ethics, then, cannot be the study of man-the-decider simply in the abstract, for there is no such man. It must be the understanding and interpretation of man's decisions and actions as responsive to God's initiative. Christian ethics is, therefore, the theory of man's response to God—of the response that he actually makes and the response that he ought to make. Its analysis must always be carried through in terms of the continuous dialogue between God and man, as that dialogue is disrupted by man's sinful rebellion and restored by God's reconciling forgiveness.

Non-Christian points of view do not know the gospel of God's revelatory and redemptive acts in and through Jesus Christ, and so they carry through their analysis from some other starting point. But for Christian ethics this is the only possible beginning and the only possible center. However, let us not conclude from this sharp disparity that Jerusalem can have nothing to do with Athens. It is, after all, for the men of Athens as well as the men of Jerusalem that God has acted. To exclude them and their viewpoints instead of taking them up within a Christian perspective would deny this and would betray the very gospel in the name of which it was proclaimed. Thus, we dare not work out our ethic by beginning with special claims about the superiority of the Christian over alien points of view. We can only begin with the gospel of God's giving himself to man, a proclamation which reveals that our being and situation—indeed those of all men—have their meaning in their dependence on and response to God's action.

2 God and Man

A DISTINCTIVE CHARACTERISTIC OF THE CHRISTIAN PERSPEC-
tive, we have seen, is the understanding that man has his very being in community with God and his fellows, a community strained toward disruption by man's acts of distrust and disobedience, yet healed by God's acts of love and reconciliation. This summary statement may seem obvious enough, but not so obvious are some of its implications for the nature of man and his relation to God. For it is implied here that man's *being* is in some significant way determined by *events*, that is, that man's very nature is historical, that to grasp what any man is, we must look at his history.

I

The meaning of this will come clearer if we reflect briefly on our actual relations with other persons. Those relations al-

ways have their character in the present because of what they
have been in the past. For example, if I call someone my
friend and take up a stance of trust and openness toward
him, this does not happen because of my arbitrary decision
in this moment to be a friend of this man. I do not find
myself easily and freely trusting, say, a perfect stranger. If
I have a friend, it is because I have *come* to have a friend,
it is because, through a series of encounters with this other
person in the past, I have gradually become acquainted
with him, and he with me, and between us has arisen the
relational reality which we call friendship. My friendship for another is thus something that arises out of the
history of my relations with that other. Precisely the same
thing is to be said of an enemy. If I call someone my
enemy, it is because my encounters with him have, far
from maturing into friendship, matured into distrust and
fear and hatred. But these realities, like friendship, have
come to be what they now are through a process of development, through a history. And given a different historical development, the present relationships would be
different realities.

It is important that we grasp a further point here. These
relations of friendship and enmity in which we stand are
not completely external to us, leaving us untouched in the
innermost core of our beings. On the contrary, it is just
such relationships that, in many respects, have made us
what we are. As I share experiences with my friend, and
he with me, we come to appreciate the aspirations, the desires, the values of each other. It is because my friend finds
real joy and satisfaction in good music, or philosophy, or
football, that he wishes me, too, to share these experiences.
And so together with him I taste of realities I had not
known before, and soon, perhaps, I share his appreciation

and joy. But this sharing occurs not only with regard to new types of experience. In our every conversation we are really exchanging experiences of the world and attitudes toward the world, and are thus coming to apprehend the world in new ways, taking up new postures toward it. My friend comes to participate in my values, attitudes, ideas, and ideals, and I in his. In short we come to participate in each other; we become, in Paul's words, "members one of another" (Rom. 12:5); the very structures of our selves come to interpenetrate each other in such a way that I am what I am because he is what he is, and because of the relationship we have come to enjoy together. Similarly, one must argue that the experiences of injury and betrayal which have given rise to relationships of distrust, fear, and enmity, are not external to my true self; they also have left their scars on what I now am; they also have shaped the structure of my self.

What we have said about friendship and enmity applies to all relationships in which we stand or have stood, relations to things as well as persons. The self is that unique kind of reality which lives in continuous responsiveness to other realities in the present, but whose very structure, from which the responses emerge, has come to be what it is because of its past. *We are our histories.* Hence, the study of history is really the unraveling backward through time of the present structures of selves, in such a way that we can see how they have come to interpenetrate each other.

The self gains its structure through history, but it is a vital and responsive reality in the present, and these two facts belong together. For to be *responsive* to another is to be one who makes himself sensitive to that other, who hears when the other speaks and who replies with relevance to what the other has said. That is, it is to be the kind of being that can adapt itself relevantly and significantly to the other reality confronting it; it is to be the kind of being that can allow itself to be shaped by the living experience of the present into some form which would not otherwise have been taken. To be responsive is, in short, to be a being for whom every present moment is a shaping moment, and thus for whom every past moment was one in which I *was* shaped, in which I was coming to have the structure which I now have. To deny that the self gains its structure through history would be to deny that it is the kind of reality which can enter into living dialogue in the present. Man's historicity—his being shaped by history—and man's finding his very being in community with others thus are two sides of the same coin; neither could be without the other.[1]

Just as history is the present structure of the self un-ravelled backward through time, so community is that structure unfolded outward so as to lay bare the interpenetration and permeation of the self with others. Thus, to speak of the communities in which we participate is to refer to the living relations to other persons which actually constitute our present being; to speak of the vital relations to other selves in which we stand is to designate the communities of which we are part. Communities are nothing but selves in living relation; selves have their very being in and through the communal relations in which they stand. Community—self—history: these are the three terms of a complex triadic relationship, none of which could exist apart from the others. Accordingly, the nature and problems of the community among men, and between man and God, must be

[1] For a treatment of man's historicity as the radically unique thing about man, and that which can most appropriately be considered the "image of God" in him, see my article, "The *Imago Dei* as Man's Historicity," *Journal of Religion* (1956) 36:157-68.

seen from three sides if they are to be properly understood. They will have their historical dimension through which they came to be what they are; they will have their personal dimension in which they must be grasped in terms of the structure and malformation of individual selves; they will have their social dimension in which we will see them as the structures and tensions in society and culture.

II

Although in developing this triadic conception of the relations of the individual, the community, and history, direct exegesis of biblical passages has not been attempted, the conception itself is directly implied in the Bible and Christian theology. For the Bible is essentially a history in and through which we can see how the situations of individual and community, each indispensable to the other, have become what they are. Moreover, it is only in terms of some such anthropology as here outlined that we can make intelligible the doctrines of the fall and sin on the one hand, and of salvation through Jesus Christ on the other. For in each of these, the claim is being made that some event in history radically shapes—in the one case for the worse, in the other for the better—our present situation.

The biblical story of the fall has many implications which we cannot explore here. However, we must note at least these two: a) The story insists that our present involvement in evil has come to us out of history, out of the past. b) The past with which we are here concerned is not merely our particular past as Americans or as Christians; it is the general human past to which all men are heir. This is emphasized through making Adam, the symbolic pro-

genitor of all men, the one through whom sinful disobedience came into human affairs.

> In Adam's fall
> We sinned all.

The evidence for these claims is so obvious that it scarcely
needs rehearsing. At every level of human intercourse
distrust, hatred, and fear rule the relations of men. This
is certainly true, for example, on the international scene
where every nation is clearly out to save itself in the full
confidence that it can trust no other. It is equally true of
the relations between white man and black both within
this country and across the globe, of the relations between
capital and labor, between the "masses" and the "eggheads,"
between Southerners and Northerners, between Protestants
and Catholics and Jews. Moreover, if we are honest, we must
admit that our personal relations likewise are filled with
often hidden, but sometimes open, distrust and hatred. All
parents far too often find moments when they cannot
stand the sight of their child, and even in other moments
they are subject to the temptation to use and manipulate
the child simply for their own ends. Children grow up in a
family atmosphere where they must continually vie for the
affection of parents and playmates. No employer hesitates
to use the threat of dismissal even with employees whom
he claims as friends, and wages and prices are never fixed
on the basis of love for all parties involved. In every
church, whatever its claims to be a community of love,
there are bitter jealousies, hatreds, and struggles for power
and influence. I need not go on. What I am referring to is
familiar to all. Our lives and our very selves are filled at
every point with poisons of distrust and fear. Who of us

is confident enough of the love of any person that he would be willing to bare absolutely and completely his every innermost thought or secret? Each of us maintains a hard protective shell against every other human for fear we might be hurt should he discover this or that secret fault or weakness which we alone know.

Now it is this fact—that human relations at every level simply are not what they ought to be—that is pointed to by the Christian doctrine of sin. That aspect of the doctrine referred to as the fall expresses the insight that we have made our communities and selves the corrupted and destructive realities they are, not just in this moment, but through history. And it is a history which ultimately includes in its corruption all men all the way back to the beginnings of the species.

On every level this is the case. Our present international problems are not just willed deliberately into being by irresponsible Communists or Americans. They are the product of a long series of events and crises stretching back through World War II, the depression, the Versailles Treaty, the Communist revolution in Russia, World War I, nineteenth-century imperialism and colonialism, the industrial revolution, and so on back to the very beginning of history. Each of these moments, though creative and productive in its own right, was shaped by the hatreds, jealousies, rivalries, and distrust which its participants held for each other. We should not be surprised, therefore, that in each of these moments seeds of evil and war were being sown which have not yet all been reaped. Moreover—and this is critical for the Christian understanding of evil—the process is self-perpetuating. For each of these events, filled with evil sown in its past, is in turn a new seed which will sprout and be harvested in some future. And so the process goes on with no foreseeable end. Clearly, it would not be possible to give a full account of present international problems without, finally, tracing them back to the beginning of human history. It is precisely this fact, that we are in the grip of a past going all the way back to the very beginning, that is indicated by the Christian doctrine of the fall.

A similar sort of analysis of the historical character of evil could be given on the individual and personal level. In my home there are three children maturing into self-hood. Do they have a real chance to become persons not infected with anxiety, hatred, and guilt? Unfortunately, no. For they are growing up in a home with parents who, however much they seek to avoid this, frequently fail them. Instead of giving them security whenever they are anxious, their parents, themselves insecure, often explode in exasperation at the children's behavior. Instead of giving them acceptance and love whenever such is needed, their parents may be conversing with a friend and resent being disturbed, or be off to the office or a dinner party to which the child has no access. Accordingly, the children learn that they must fend for themselves, that they cannot fully trust even their parents, that life is often hard and cruel and unloving. And they may well resent this and become filled with unhappiness, bitterness, and hatred. Is it their fault if they then become self-centered, hateful persons? What else could they become in such a setting? Have they not been trapped into it at the very moments of their lives when they were young and tender and defenseless, when they bruised easily? Certainly they do not bear sole responsibility for the distortions in their personalities. But neither can their parents be held entirely responsible. For the parents themselves have become what they are, weak, inadequate, insecure, distrustful, because of the home situations in which they matured. And so on ad infinitum. Clearly, the evils in personal lives are handed on from generation to generation almost like a dread hereditary disease, though the transmission here is primarily social, not biological. To understand these evils there is no stopping with this generation or that; we must push all the way back to the beginnings if we are to have a full and adequate interpretation.

The Christian doctrine of the fall is the vivid expression of the fact that, however much human evil may have its present locus in our distorted selves and diseased communities, it has in a certain sense been foisted upon us by a history which we have not chosen but from which we cannot escape, a history going back to the beginning of the human species, to Adam.

III

It is in this corrupted history, according to the gospel, that God has acted in and through Jesus Christ to free man from his bondage to sin and evil. What, now, was this action of God? Was it an action in which he laid down the proper laws of human conduct, for example, in the Sermon on the Mount? Was it an action through which he gave us an example, in Jesus of Nazareth, of how we ought to live? Was it an action in which he appeased his own wrath by sacrifice of his son? We cannot adequately understand the action of God in Jesus Christ simply by reciting such well-worn formulas as these. Only through seeing it in the context of the whole history reported in the Bible can we grasp what is involved.

There is not time to review the full movement of Old

Testament history, but we must touch on a few high points. It is generally agreed by Old Testament scholars that the great turning-point of Israel's history occurred probably during the thirteenth century, B.C., with the series of events that included the exodus from Egypt and the covenant with God at Mt. Sinai. For it was in and through these events that the Hebrews bound themselves to their God, and he to them. Yahweh would be their God; they would be his people. Throughout the invasion of Canaan, the wars with the Philistines, the long struggle with Canaanite baal religion, and finally the destruction of the two kingdoms and the exile, it was the memory of the covenant with Yahweh that provided a thread of continuity in terms of which the prophets and others could interpret the real meaning of what was happening to Israel.

The great creative writer, "J," known to us through the careful researches of modern historians, produced (around 950 B.C.) a history of Israel—the first great piece of historical writing anywhere and the nucleus of the Old Testament. In it he made two things especially clear: a) That it was Yahweh, the God of the Hebrews, who created the world, and who continues to work toward the realization of his own purposes in the world; and b) That this God, who is the source of all existence and works in and through all of history, acted in a special way in Hebrew history, making a covenant with Israel, the chosen agent of his purposes. In the light of J's important historical work the great prophets of the eighth century—Amos, Hosea, Micah, and Isaiah—found it possible to interpret contemporary historical events as also the expression of the purposes of God. The movements of Assyria against Israel and Judah, said Isaiah, are not due simply to the imperialistic designs of the Assyrian king. Rather they are instrumentalities of

the judgment of Yahweh upon the Israelites who have failed
to keep their side of the covenant.

> Ah, Assyria, the rod of my anger,
>   the staff of my fury!
> Against the godless nation I send him,
>   and against the people of my wrath I
>   command him. (Isa. 10:5-6)

In the light of their awareness that in Israel's injustice,
apostasy, and degeneracy the purposes of God were not
being fulfilled, the prophets looked forward to a day in
the future—the Day of the Lord (Amos 5:18-20; Isa. 2:
12-22, 13:6-16; etc.)—when God's rule over all history
would be fully manifest in destruction of his enemies, and
his will would finally be done. All of history—past, present,
future—was in the hands of God, and the course of history
was moving inexorably toward the fulfillment of his purpose
to establish perfectly his kingdom. However, because history had become the domain of sinful rebellion against
God, it seemed clear this great event could happen only
if God were to intervene directly, perhaps overturning the
powers now loose in history (as men like Zephaniah,
Zechariah, Joel, and others thought), perhaps through
transforming the evil heart of man from "stone" into
"flesh" (as Ezekiel declared), perhaps through entering into
a "new covenant" with man (as Jeremiah hoped). But surely the kingdom of God, that great transformation and
fulfillment of all history, will come, and then even

The wolf shall dwell with the lamb,
  and the leopard shall lie down with the kid,
and the calf and the lion and the fatling together,
  and a little child shall lead them.

The cow and the bear shall feed;
  their young shall lie down together;
  and the lion shall eat straw like the ox.
The sucking child shall play over the hole of the asp,
  and the weaned child shall put his hand on the adder's den.
They shall not hurt or destroy
  in all my holy mountain;
for the earth shall be full of the knowledge of the Lord
  as the waters cover the sea. (Isa. 11:6-9)

The Old Testament period moves forward toward its end in a rising crescendo of hope. The expectation of the mighty act of God which will transform everything into the fulfillment of his purposes is the dominant theme in the years immediately preceding the Christian era.

It is in this context of hope and expectation that the New Testament must be understood and the significance of Jesus Christ apprehended. For the New Testament writers were convinced that precisely this hope was fulfilled in Christ. The long historical preparation recorded in the Old Testament had finally borne fruit in the appearance of an itinerant preacher and healer, Jesus of Nazareth, and particularly in his death and resurrection. Jesus himself had come preaching that "The time is fulfilled, and the kingdom of God is at hand" (Mark 1:15); his powers of healing seemed to him and his disciples clear evidence that the kingdom was already in their midst (Luke 11:20; 17:21). Although Jesus' execution as a common criminal appeared to call into question the validity of this conviction, it was not long before they became convinced that God had raised him from the dead, fully vindicating his message and unequivocally designating him as the one who was to establish the kingdom among men (cf. Rom. 1:4).

The long expected New Age, then, was *now here*, and it was known to Jesus' followers! God's decisive action in history through which he was overthrowing the power of evil and sin was actually in process! The new covenant between God and man, which Jeremiah had expected, was now established, and men were being given the new hearts for which Ezekiel had hoped. The kingdom of God was here, and men were being called to live in it!

A scattered selection of passages, characteristic of the New Testament as a whole, underlines the point: "the kingdom of God has come upon you" (Matt. 12:28); "this is what was spoken by the prophet" (Acts 2:16); "He has delivered us from the dominion of darkness and transferred us to the kingdom of his beloved Son" (Col. 1:13); "if any one is in Christ, he is a new creation; the old has passed away, behold, the new has come" (II Cor. 5:17); "You have been born anew, not of perishable seed but of imperishable" (I Pet. 1:23); "the darkness is passing away and the true light is already shining . . . it is the last hour" (I John 2:8, 18). Thus the long expected dramatic intervention of God in human history—the great Day of the Lord—had begun with Jesus' ministry, was certified with his resurrection, and was soon to be completed with his expected return on the clouds of heaven as the Son of Man. The earliest Christians were men who knew themselves to be living "between the times"—between the *beginning* of the final transformation of all of history, and its *completion*.

The deepest significance of the New Testament for Christian ethics is not to be found in its moral teachings, nor in Jesus' example of good behavior, nor in some dogma about a divine transaction changing God's attitude toward us. It is to be found rather in its presentation of God's

mighty act of sacrifice without reservation (Phil. 2)
through which his faithful love and forgiveness of man became both visible and effective in human history, establishing the kingdom of God. As Paul puts it, "while we were
yet sinners" and his "enemies we were reconciled to God by
the death of his Son" (Rom. 5:8, 10). "In this the love of
God was made manifest among us," says the writer of
I John, "that God sent his only Son into the world, so that
we might live through him" (4:9). This new awareness
of the presence of God's love in their midst freed the first
Christians of their doubts and fears. No longer had man
to live a self-centered existence, always building walls between himself and others for protection against betrayals
and hurts, for it was now clear that God—the very foundation of all existence—is absolutely trustworthy; he never
betrays. So man, also, could take the risk of loving God
and his fellows without reservation. Thus God's act of love,
in making it possible for man to love, literally transformed
him into a "new creation" (II Cor. 5:17) no longer centered in himself but centered instead in God. And thus it
became possible for human lives to manifest God's love,
for human love to become the vehicle in history and
society of the divine love.

From this brief résumé of the biblical story, it should
be clear that God's action in Christ was not an event isolated or separated from the rest of history. On the contrary, it was the moment in which God's activity in every
moment of history came to sharp focus. The entire Old
Testament is the story of God's loving preparation and
education of a people—who originally thought of him as
essentially a God of war and violence—so that they could
apprehend him as one whose nature is love. Thus, from the
creation until the appearance of Jesus Christ, God in his love

was working with man, preparing the way, so that finally he could break into human history decisively as love. Again, the history of the church since Jesus Christ is the story of the spreading of this message and fact of God's love through all history to all people. Jesus Christ is the center, the focal point of history, through which has been revealed the ultimate fact of history: that it rests in the will and purposes of a loving God. In this sense Jesus Christ is the supreme act of God. It is to this action, through which the divine love flows into human history and becomes a fact within history, that we are called to respond.

IV

If the history reported in the Bible be accepted as revealing the nature and purposes of the ultimate reality with which we have to do—and Christian faith makes just this affirmation—then the moral context in which we live and act is not defined exclusively by the corrupted sinful history in which we are living. On the contrary, the most significant reality which we confront is not human sin but the God who acts to redeem us from that sin. Whereas the analysis of man's sinfulness taken by itself might lead us to despair of any possibility for real community among men, the revelation that God himself, creator of the heavens and the earth, is working in love to extricate man from his plight, restores hope for man and for human history. For "If God be for us, who can be against us?" (Rom. 8:31 KJV.) Doubtless sin and rebellion are still with us, but now we know that this empirical state of human existence is not the last word.

It is necessary to sketch out a bit further the implications of this fact for ethics. Right action must now be understood in relation to God's redemptive activity: What is the proper response to the God who loves? The answer is given in summary in the first letter of John and in words of Jesus: "Beloved, if God so loved us, we also ought to love one another" (I John 4:11). "You shall love the Lord your God with all your heart . . . [and] you shall love your neighbor as yourself." (Mark 12:30-31.) We must give ourselves in service to our neighbors, as God sacrifices himself for us. The radical demands this obligation lays upon us we will consider in later chapters. For now we must see certain broader implications of the fact that our love is called forth by God's love.

In the first place, it must be emphasized that our love is in *response* to God's love. As we noted earlier, man's problem is precisely that he is imprisoned within walls of distrust, fear, self-interest, and guilt. Therefore, he neither really desires, nor is he able, freely to give himself in love to neighbor and enemy. Only as God frees us to love, by giving himself to us in love, are we enabled to act out of the conviction that the ultimate reality with which we have to do is love, and sustains us for love. As we are freed from fears about our own security and enabled to trust that he who created us will sustain and forgive us, it becomes possible for us to love and serve others with a new spontaneity and creativity. It even begins to be possible to love those who hate and distrust us; we come to know ourselves as called to lives of reconciling and redemptive action among our fellows. For to be truly responsive to God's action, our activity must be modeled after God's own act in Jesus Christ, in which "While we were [still his] enemies we were reconciled to God by the death of his Son" (Rom. 5:10). We must, therefore, devote ourselves to restoring the broken community among men if we would respond to God the Reconciler.

In the second place, we must remember that the one who reconciles us to himself in Jesus Christ is none other than our creator and the creator of all that exists. Our response to God, then, cannot be in relation only to God's reconciling activity; we must also be responsive to him as Creator, the one who out of his love has brought the world into being. A loving response here begins with acknowledgment of the goodness of existence as God has made it. We must not begrudge being just the persons he has made us, nor the place in time and space where he has set us; we must willingly take our part in the created order, rejoicing in the goodness of God's world. We must love that world, seeking to know it better, so that we can more readily find our proper place in it. The artist's search for and appreciation of the beauty in God's creation, and the scientist's and scholar's search for truth about the universe, are indispensable dimensions of man's proper response to the goodness of the created order. Schweitzer has popularized the conviction that we should express "reverence for life"; if we would truly respond to God as Creator, we must have reverence for all of creation, reverence for being.[2]

Finally, we must say that for the Christian faith he who has brought us into being and has revealed himself as reconciling love is also continuously present to all his creation, working out his purposes in it and revealing himself to it. If we are to respond to God, we must also respond to him as Holy Spirit, present in every event of history, providentially ordering it according to his loving purposes. This requires

[2] Cf. H. Richard Niebuhr *Radical Monotheism and Western Culture* (New York: Harper, 1960), pp. 31-37.

us to look for God's hand in everything that happens to us. We will see his blessings in those things which seem to us undeserved goods. In those events which frustrate us, we will see his love judging and restraining our sinful ways. In the struggles of our social existence—e.g., the tensions between the United States and Russia on the international scene—as well as in our personal affairs, we will always seek to respond to God's providential ordering of the course of history. In every happening it is God's loving hand which we must discern and to which we must respond, for the God of Christian faith is also the Holy Spirit, living and active in every moment.

Our response to the God who loves must be characterized then by all three of these dimensions: response to him as Redeemer and Reconciler, as Creator, and as living, governing Spirit. For it is the one trinitarian God whose love has come to us in Jesus Christ.

We can now see that the Christian moral life cannot be simply a life of imitation of Jesus nor a life guided by some eternal principles supposedly embodied in the Ten Commandments or in Jesus' teachings. For it is a life most fundamentally defined by its context and source: God's action—a reality first apprehended in our dawning awareness of his act in Jesus Christ, but continuously present with us in every moment. And it finds its fulfillment in our free response, new and creative in every moment, searching for his will for that moment. Christian faith—faith in the God who reveals himself in Jesus Christ—is the presupposition of the Christian moral life; the Christian life is the product and outworking of Christian faith. Christian ethics is the attempt to understand and interpret this continuous dialogue between God's action and our response.

3 The Church and the World

"God was in Christ reconciling the world to himself, not counting their trespasses against them, and entrusting to us the message of reconciliation. So we are ambassadors for Christ, God making his appeal through us."
(II Cor. 5:19-20)

R IGHT ACTION, FROM THE PERSPECTIVE OF CHRISTIAN FAITH, begins not with man's aspirations and desires but with God's act in Jesus Christ. Men's desires and aims gain their character from the historical situation in which they emerge, but human history itself—and therefore the communities that arise within it—has become distorted and confused and the bearer of evil powers of distrust and hatred. These powers in turn perpetuate themselves through shaping the character of the persons and communities which emerge within the context of history, and transmitting that history to future generations. Thus man's situation is a vicious one from which he cannot extricate himself. But the claim of the Christian gospel is that God, out of his unfailing mercy and gracious love, has broken through the shell of unfaith and lovelessness by himself coming to man in the person of Jesus Christ, bringing forgiveness and reconciliation, healing the wounds of estrangement among men and between man and God. Right action therefore begins with appropriate response to God's action of love. The good life is nothing else than the life of love and self-giving elicited from us as we become aware of God's loving sacrifice for us. To live in response to God is thus to become a channel to our fellow men of the same love and self-giving with which God came to us; it is, in short, to become "ambassadors for Christ" through whom God's reconciling love makes its appeal to our fellows. "He who loves is born of God and knows God. He who does not love does not know God; for God is love." (I John 4:7-8.)

What, now, is this love that is at once required and made possible by God's act of condescension and self-giving in Christ? There is no question that for the Christian faith the ultimate model or picture in terms of which Christian love must be understood is God's own act of self-giving through coming to man in history and ultimately, despite man's rejection, reconciling man to himself. "In this is love," says the first letter of John, "not that we loved God but that he loved us" (4:10). Here, then, is the final norm of Christian ethics in terms of which all else must be understood. But this model, this picture, this norm, may itself, when interpreted as the standard in terms of which I am to order my conduct, seem abstract and irrelevant and almost unreal.

I

God loves me, we say, and I should love my neighbor in response—but what does this really tell me about how I should govern the details of my life? What, after all, does this tell me about the vocation I should choose, or whom I should marry, or whether I should buy a new car this year? The decisions I have to make from day to day are small and concrete. How does the bare fact of the Christian claim that God loves me, forgives me, reconciles me to himself, affect these decisions? The fact that many different and even contradictory ways of understanding the Christian's situation in society have appeared in Christian history is evidence enough that the implications of God's love for concrete behavior are by no means clear and unambiguous.

Radical Christian groups such as the Reformation Anabaptists have always insisted that the right interpretation of these implications is to be found in the teachings of Jesus. Here is set forth in the most radical form what God's love requires in our relations with our fellows, and this picture is fully consistent with the self-giving, self-sacrificial, reconciling love of God which is proclaimed in the Christian gospel. If Christians have been all too willing to say that Jesus' ethic is an ethic that applies to God's coming kingdom but not to this present world, or is appropriate for monks but not for the great mass of ordinary Christians, or applies to personal life but not the social order, or if they have otherwise "watered down" the terrible implications of Jesus' understanding of God's will, it is only because they have felt that the burden here laid on us is more than we can bear. That is, they have tended to answer the question of how we ought to respond to God in terms of their own notions of human possibilities, rather than simply by reference to God's revelation of himself and the radicalness of his love. But we have seen that we dare not thus begin with man: we must rather begin by accepting the authority of God's revelation to reshape our every conception of human possibility. We must, then, take very seriously the claim of the Anabaptist-Mennonite tradition that the radical sayings of Jesus set before us a clear picture of the ethical import of God's act, and that here is portrayed precisely the kind of conduct required in our relations with our fellows.

What, now, was Jesus' teaching regarding our relations to others? We have not time here, nor is it necessary, to analyze his teachings in detail. It is well known that Jesus' activity centered in the conviction that the kingdom of God was coming, indeed, was already present in his ministry. All of Jesus' teaching and action were governed by this expectation and awareness of the presence of the kingdom. And this fact, in turn, rendered every other consideration irrelevant. "No one can serve two masters" (Matt. 6:24), so it was necessary to distinguish very clearly between all human interests and values and God's demands. Even the basic needs of life were unimportant in the face of the demand to participate in the kingdom.

Therefore do not be anxious, saying, "What shall we eat?" or "What shall we drink?" or "What shall we wear?" For the Gentiles seek all these things; and your heavenly Father knows that you need them all. But seek first his kingdom and his righteousness. (Matt. 6:31-33)

Indeed, one must be willing to give up anything and everything for the kingdom of God.

The kingdom of heaven is like treasure hidden in a field, which a man found and covered up; then in his joy he goes and sells all that he has and buys that field. Again, the kingdom of heaven is like a merchant in search of fine pearls, who, on finding one pearl of great value, went and sold all that he had and bought it. (Matt. 13:44-45)

It is not enough merely to give up material blessings of this life for the kingdom; we must even be ready to sacrifice our own bodies if they stand in the way of obedience.

If your hand causes you to sin, cut it off; it is better for you to enter life maimed than with two hands to go to hell. . . . And if your foot causes you to sin, cut it off; it is better for you to enter life lame than with two feet to be thrown into hell. And if your eye causes you to sin, pluck it out; it is better for you to enter the kingdom of God with one eye than with two eyes to be thrown into hell. (Mark 9:43-47)

Thus the demand laid upon us is absolute. We must be willing to give up any and every tie to human values and goods for God's kingdom. The first requirement laid on man is to decide, to say *no* to self and to everything that belongs to the self, and to say *yes* to God's demands, however radical or impossible they may appear to be.

The radicalness of these demands comes out most clearly, perhaps, in the great series of antitheses found in the fifth chapter of Matthew. Jesus is here portrayed as rejecting certain of the basic commandments of the Jewish Torah. We must remember that the Torah, as interpreted by the Pharisees and others of Jesus' time, was understood as prescribing the kind of behavior appropriate in every conceivable situation. The complex legalistic interpretations did not grow out of some perverse obtuseness of Jews trying to obscure God's will; on the contrary, it grew out of their conscientious efforts to discover and apply God's will for every situation in which a first-century Jew might find himself. In view of this, it is important for us to note that Jesus rejects the Torah as thus interpreted, not because it is made to cover every aspect of life, i.e., not because it is too strict, but rather because it is *not strict enough*, not far-reaching enough in its penetration into all aspects of human existence (cf. Matt. 23:23). Listen to Jesus' words:

You have heard that it was said to the men of old, "You shall not kill; and whoever kills shall be liable to judgment." But I say to you that every one who is angry with his brother shall be liable to judgment; whoever insults his brother shall be liable to the council, and whoever says, "You fool!" shall be liable to the hell of fire. . . .

You have heard that it was said, "You shall not commit adultery." But I say to you that every one who looks at a woman lustfully has already committed adultery with her in his heart. . . .

You have heard that it was said, "An eye for an eye and a tooth for a tooth." But I say to you, Do not resist one who is evil. But if any one strikes you on the right cheek, turn to him the other also; and if any one would sue you and take your coat, let him have your cloak as well; and if any one forces you to go one mile, go with him two miles. Give to him who begs from you, and do not refuse him who would borrow from you.

You have heard that it was said, "You shall love your neighbor and hate your enemy." But I say to you, Love your enemies and pray for those who persecute you, so that you may be sons of your Father who is in heaven; for he makes his sun rise on the evil and on the good, and sends rain on the just and on the unjust. (Matt. 5:21-22, 27-28, 38-45)

If you love those who love you, what credit is that to you? For

even sinners love those who love them. And if you do good to
those who do good to you, what credit is that to you? For even
sinners do the same. And if you lend to those from whom you
hope to receive, what credit is that to you? Even sinners lend
to sinners, to receive as much again. But love your enemies, and
do good, and lend, expecting nothing in return; and your reward will be great, and you will be sons of the Most High; for
he is kind to the ungrateful and the selfish. (Luke 6:32-35)

The thing for us to note here is the absoluteness, indeed
the *impossibleness*, of Jesus' demands. The old law had
held murder to be wrong. Jesus does not challenge that
judgment. But to think that working out elaborate legal defi-
nitions of murder and then staying within the letter of the
law is to fulfill God's will is simply foolishness. It is not
the murderer alone who transgresses God's command; anyone who feels and expresses anger "shall be liable to judgment." Or take the matter of adultery. The mere presence
of illicit sexual desire, however unexpressed, however deep-
ly hidden in the heart, is violation of God's holy will. And
what of our relations to our enemies, to those whom we
dislike and who mistreat us? Toleration is the very most
that can rightly be expected here, we might well think; if
we do not repay them with the coin they give us, surely
no more is required. But no! Jesus insists we should *love*
our enemies, we should do positive good to those who harm
us, we should give aid and comfort to those who would destroy us. It is not enough that we refrain from violation of
the law—even Jesus' stringent interpretations of the laws
regarding murder and adultery—however impossible that
might seem; it is not enough that our relations with friends
and loved ones be characterized by perfect love; it is not
enough that we tolerate our enemies, however difficult that
might be: we are to love perfectly, not simply those who

love us, but those who hate us! A more extreme demand
than this could scarcely be imagined. A demand more impossible of fulfillment could hardly be laid upon us who
find it difficult even to love our friends.

But, after all, God makes his sun to shine and his rain
to fall on good and evil alike; he shows no partiality to
those who love and obey him. He loves all and blesses all.
Those who do not know the love of God might have
some excuse for not loving their enemies. But Jesus' disciples, knowing God's love and forgiveness of the low-
liest and most rebellious of sinners seeking to destroy his
kingdom, have no excuse for treating their enemies otherwise than with a similar love. "You, therefore," as Matthew
sums it up, "must be perfect, as your heavenly Father is
perfect" (5:48).

II

Jesus' ethic is the ethic of the kingdom of God. As such,
it is a description of the character of the community which
is ruled by God's love and through which God's love becomes empirical reality shaping the actual interpersonal relations of human beings here on earth. It is important
to note this is an ethic for the church militant, not
simply for the church triumphant. It is taken for granted
that those to whom Jesus is speaking are in a situation not
favorable to their existence or their views: they must deal
with "enemies," but they are to "love" them. Indeed, it is
precisely in this loving of the enemies (of themselves and
even of God) that they become "sons" of God (Luke
6:35; Matt. 5:44-45; cf. I John 4), i.e., living members of
his household and kingdom, who are vehicles of God's love
in human history. The community of reconciliation to which

Jesus' followers belong is thus the cutting edge of God's love bringing redemption to rebellious men in sinful human history (II Cor. 5:19-20).

The radical demands of Jesus' ethical teachings are obviously consistent with the fundamental claim of the Christian gospel, that in Jesus Christ God himself really has broken and is breaking into human history, transforming man's sinful existence with his redemptive love. If there were no actual community of living men in which the wounds of distrust, unfaithfulness and hatred were in fact being healed through forgiveness and reconciling love, it is hard to see how the gospel of God's love could be anything more than an abstract and empty pronouncement—a far cry from the "good news" of the real transformative power of God's love in human lives proclaimed by the earliest Christians. Jesus' ethical teachings express in the most concrete terms the way in which God's love becomes an actual fact in the lives of men and women. It becomes an empirical historical reality as and when human beings forgive and become reconciled with their enemies, not in the sense of some pious, martyred turning of the other cheek, but so that the enemy knows he has met in this person the very love of God. Those of us to whom God's love has been made known through the death of his Son are commanded to love our enemies so that they, too, can say with us and with Paul, "while we were enemies we were reconciled" (Rom. 5:10).

We can now see what the church is and must be for the perspective of Christian faith. It is nothing else than the community of reconciliation through which God's love is penetrating human history. It is the historical community in which God's love is known as real, and which therefore manifests forgiving and reconciling love toward its own historical enemies. It is the point within sinful and warring human history where the disloyalty and faithlessness characteristic of human affairs is actually being overcome by faith and hope and love. Christian faith believes this church—at the front line of battle being waged within God's kingdom by rebels against his love—will ultimately take up within herself the world now in rebellion against God; thus her destiny is finally to become God's perfect kingdom. But at present the church is in no position to make any such claims to perfection or completeness. Although the church knows in the present—and this is the very presence of Christ's spirit within her—"a foretaste of the future" (Rom. 8:23 Goodspeed), her life here and now is one of suffering and inner struggle as she waits "for the sons of God to be disclosed" and for her own members "to be declared God's sons" (Rom. 8:19, 23 Goodspeed). The church must ever live oriented toward the future then, toward this expected fulfillment. Her present existence falls within the early stages of the great transformation, but these do not have their real meaning unless and until their completion is realized (cf. Phil. 3:12-14). This is why Paul can deny the present fulfillment of the church's life and mission to the point of saying, finally, that it is in "hope we were saved" (Rom. 8:24).

III

We cannot here work out a full doctrine of the church, however important that might be to a fully developed Christian ethic. We can only sketch some of the implications for Christian ethics of the historical and theological fact of the church's reality. The church's significance for ethics derives from the fact that she is at the front lines of God's transforming of human existence through his redemptive love. Indeed, we might say the church is the very process of that transformation; she is the world being transformed. This means that the church can never separate herself from the world and remain the church. For the church's very reality lies in her being the point where God's love is overcoming man's rebellion.

Once you were no people but now you are God's people; once you had not received mercy but now you have received mercy. . . . You are a chosen race, a royal priesthood, a holy nation, God's own people, *that you may declare the wonderful deeds* of him who called you out of darkness into his marvelous light. (I Peter 2:10, 9, italics mine.)

For the church to attempt to separate herself from man's rebellion through separating herself from rebellious men would be to dissolve her own reality. She would destroy herself externally through forsaking her true task, the overcoming of man's rebellion wherever found; and she would destroy herself internally by her supposition, incompatible with Christian humility, that sin and uncleanness reside principally in those from whom she has departed and not within her own members. But "If we say we have no sin, we deceive ourselves, and the truth is not in us. If we confess our sins, he is faithful and just, and will forgive our sins and cleanse us from all unrighteousness." (I John 1:8-9.) The church is never in a position to make claims for herself, least of all, claims of her own sinlessness or perfection, for her very being lies in the acknowledgment that we are saved through the power of *God's* love, not through something that we ourselves are or might become. "We have this treasure in earthen vessels, to show that the transcendent power belongs to God and not to us." (II Cor. 4:7.)

The church, then, the community in which God's love is known to be real, can never afford to separate herself from the world, for her mission to the world is of her very essence. This is the basis of the missionary and evangelistic impulse without which a community cannot be Christian.[1] It is not at all clear, however, that our usual missionary efforts—sending a few people to "foreign lands" or "heathen peoples" while the church at home remains a stable community with no real outreach to her own environment—are much more than a way of avoiding the demand to be an effective mission in the world.

The fact that the church is the process of transformation of the world means that no sharp distinction between church and world can be sustained. A process of change always participates in both realities, that *from* which the change is occurring and that *toward* which it is moving. A naturalized citizen does not immediately give up everything from the old country and take on all the customs of the new, and it is always impossible to draw a sharp line setting off those who have decisively taken up the new way of life from those who have retained the old. We may well be "free citizens of Heaven" (Phil. 3:20 Weymouth), but we still live on earth and we await the final transformation in which our citizenship will be realized. The terms "church" and "world," therefore, do not stand so much for static realities posed over against each other, each sharply

[1] It should be noted in passing that early Anabaptism was a missionary movement in just this sense—perhaps the first modern missionary movement—attempting to spread the love of God everywhere. See, e.g., F. H. Littell, "The Anabaptist Theology of Missions," *Mennonite Quarterly Review* (1947), 21:5-17. S. F. Pannabecker, "Missions, Foreign Mennonite," *Mennonite Encyclopedia* (Scottdale, Pa.: Mennonite Publishing House, 1955-59), 3:712-17.

definable, as for terminals in the living process of history in which we exist. "World" refers to that condition of sin and rebellion from which we are being changed through God's love; "church" refers to that community of love into which we are being moved. In this sense the church really exists only eschatologically, as the goal of history, the realization of the kingdom of God, that which is to come when God's purposes are finally and fully realized, that for which we hope and pray and for which we live.

Without this hope and expectation and confidence that God is actually changing this world into his kingdom of love, it would be meaningless and absurd for us to give our lives in absolute self-sacrifice and love. Within the context of this hope, however, such self-giving makes sense, for then it can be seen as the very process through which the transformation of human existence is coming about. The actual churches in which we live are in the world, and the world is in them as well, and therefore no clear line between church and world can be drawn. But the eschatological church, which is taking up the world into herself and transforming it into the community of the love of God, is also present in our actual churches, and through them in the world, and it is for this reality which is to come—a "foretaste" being already present—that we live and move and have our being as men who love others in response to God's love.

IV

What, now, has all this to do with the concrete problems of right and wrong, with the decisions we must make daily? We have been describing in theological terms the *context* of the Christian life, the situation in which all decisions and actions occur and which should be present to our minds whenever we act. There are three essential factors in this context, none of which can be ignored. The first of course is God's act. Christian action must always be response to the gospel, a response of gratitude to God for his love. It should be clear by now that this act of God's love is not something concentrated exclusively on a particular point in past time, the appearance of Jesus of Nazareth in history. Although it is true that in a decisive way God's love broke into human history with Jesus Christ, it is necessary to go on and say that this was but a crucial beginning point of the process intended to culminate in the final establishment of God's kingdom of love among all men. God's act of love first becomes incarnate in human history with Jesus Christ, but it does not end there; it continues to work in and through human history until the end, when it reaches its completion. It is a historical act and thus takes time, as all historical acts do, but it is a historical act that ultimately will take up all of history into itself. God's act in Christ will not be completed, therefore, until the end of history has come.

This means that we in human history are living "between the times"—between the appearance of Christ and the end of the world, between the historical beginning of God's mighty act of salvation and its completion. We live in the period of transformation, the period in which God's love is an active force in human history: we live in the time of the church. For the Christian community, all decisions and actions must be governed by this consciousness that God has begun his great act of love, is even now acting, and shall finally establish his kingdom. This is the ultimate cosmic fact, the real truth about the universe and about history in terms of which all else must be judged. We are not to take our bearings simply from the empirical historical situation in which we find ourselves. Not even the ideals, ideas, values and goals which we can discern in our situation are to be the basis in terms of which we orient our lives. Instead our lives must be oriented toward the past—God's historical act of self-giving in Jesus Christ, and the future—his final establishment of a community of love. For Christian ethics, right and wrong cannot be decided merely in terms of the present situation in history, however impregnated with ideals our situation may appear to be. For the Christian ethic is historical-eschatological: it takes its bearings, not from what seems real and obvious in the present, but from the living past and the hoped for future.

Moreover, the Christian ethic, eschatological to the core, makes sense only from a point of view which does not judge things in terms of the possibilities or probabilities of the present but believes rather in God's ultimate triumph. It is this expectation that enables the Christian ethic to express itself in radical nonresistance. We saw before that in Jesus' teaching unequivocal love of enemies is required; indeed, it is in such self-giving that God's love becomes historically concrete. But self-sacrifice to enemies is both absurd and imprudent in any but an eschatological perspective. There is no reason to suppose that in history—in your life and mine—such love will always, or even usually, result in the transformation of enemies into friends. In its most notable exemplification it resulted in crucifixion. On any short-term view it should be obvious that power, not love, rules human history, that those who love and give themselves are only destroyed. "Pragmatic pacifism" is thus nonsense. But the Christian ethic is not rooted in any short-term judgments of this sort. It is rooted in an eschatological perspective in which the ultimate overcoming of the world by the power of God's love is expected. From this perspective, absolute self-giving makes sense. For faith, believing that God's purpose will prevail, it is possible, indeed only reasonable, to express that purpose through love, even though this means historical destruction. But this is true only for a faith that lives in this hope, not for any other perspective.

Thus, when we say that Christian ethics is founded in faith in God's act, we are making a most radical kind of statement with the most radical kind of consequences. It means very literally that "we look not to the things that are [or can be] seen [in this our present life] but to the things that are unseen; for the things that are seen are transient, but the things that are unseen are eternal" (II Cor. 4:18). Right and wrong are not to be defined in terms of any utilitarian consequences, any human ideals or aspirations, any human desires or needs. They are to be defined only in terms of God's will and God's act of love even to enemies, in the confidence that finally God's purpose will prevail.

The context in which we act, however, is not exhaustively described simply by referring thus to God's act. God's purpose is for history and his act is in history as the presence of the historical community called the church. The actual situation and struggles of the church in and with the world are therefore the sociological dimensions of the context. There is no such thing as an individual Christian responding to God's act in isolation. The call to Christian faith always comes through the historical activity of the church; the love of God is always mediated to us through the actual love of other persons—parents, children, friends, teachers; our faith comes to us through the work of the church in history. Nor is it possible to respond to God's love in isolated individuality. For to respond to God's love is to serve our fellows with love, to become the vehicle through which God's love flows to them. God's love thus always comes to us through human community and it necessarily leads us back into human community. The church, we have seen, is just that community whose special historical mission is to witness to God's love and to be the channel through which that love flows into the world. Thus, response to God's love means entering into the church and its task of being the mediator of love to the world. There is no such thing as a Christian solitary: a Christian is inevitably involved in the work of the church.

V

We have thus far been discussing the nature of the church as though it were perfectly obvious just what historical community we were attempting to describe. But this is not the case. There are numerous communities claiming to be *the* church or a church. They have different, and even contradictory, conceptions and interpretations of their nature and mission. To what, then, are we actually referring when we speak of the church? We cannot here give a full theological description of the marks of the church, but at least this much must be said. It is necessary to be clear in our minds whether we are speaking *eschatologically* or *empirically* about the church. (This distinction is the more appropriate historicist form of what is sometimes called, in Platonic terms, the distinction between the "invisible" and "visible" church.) If we are speaking eschatologically of the church, the church is all mankind transformed into God's kingdom. Though the eschatological church is not now visible to our eyes, it is in the hope and expectation that God is working in history toward this end —however problematic this may appear from within history —that is at the heart of Christian faith. All of the forces of history are finally, in God's providence, being directed toward this end, though this can be seen only by God himself and believed only by faith; to the eye of the "natural man" the historical evidence hardly appears to warrant such high hope.

There is a community within history, however, which lives by just this hope. That community is the empirical church which knows herself, in faith, to have as her ultimate destiny nothing less than becoming God's perfect community of love. The empirical church thus consists of those who consciously and conscientiously live in response to God's act in Jesus Christ and in expectation of his ultimate transformation of all of human history. It is difficult to see, from this point of view, how the empirical church can be anything but a confessional "believers' church." In this, also, the Anabaptist "sectarians" appear to have been correct. There may be a sense in which all men are in the church, as the "church-type" churches [2] have maintained, and have symbolized through infant baptism. But if so, this becomes a reality only in the eschaton; it is not an empirical reality in our present historical existence as the church-type churches have in effect claimed. The actual historical community, through which God's love in Jesus Christ is mediated to the world, is that community of believers who have been seized by that love and in turn seek to respond

[2] For the classical statement of the distinction between "church" and "sect" see Ernst Troeltsch, *The Social Teaching of the Christian Churches*. Trans. Olive Wyon (London: Allen & Unwin, 1931), esp. Vol. II.

to it through giving themselves as fully as they can in service to both neighbor and enemy.[3]

If the empirical church—the actual historical community through which God's love is moving into the "world"—is a believers' church, then we must take seriously certain implications. In the first place, it will be necessary for the church to realize that she is the *empirical*, not the eschatological, church (except by anticipation). That is, she is a church very much involved in the struggle to overcome the world and in consequence a church in which her relations to the world are always ambiguous. She can never claim to render judgment with God's mind; she can only claim to be a community of humble believers living by God's forgiveness and love. She must always recognize, therefore, that her judgments are *human* judgments, and as such are infected with shortsightedness and relativity, to say nothing of pride and sin. Even, nay especially! her judgments of her own nature and mission are of that character. She lives by the *hope* of becoming, in the eschaton, the true expression of God's will, but she knows that she is still engaged in the battle with the world at every point. She lives in her mission to bring God's love to the "world," but she recognizes that her judgment even about who or what is the "world" is finite and full of error. The empirical church must always seek out what she can call

[3] It might be well to observe here that in the light of this stringent "Anabaptist" view of the church, modern Mennonite churches—with their staid, bourgeois memberships, their comfortable adjustment to laissez-faire capitalist practices, their regular practice of baptizing the young when they complete catechism class whether they have mature Christian convictions or not, their unwillingness to practice any kind of significant church discipline—are very little different in actuality from Christian groups of the "church-type" tradition.

the "world" and there bring her ministrations of love and service, but she must reckon with her own limitations in making all of these judgments.

This means that the empirical church will realize that she defines herself, and the world over against her where she must work, largely in pragmatic terms. The church defines her own membership pragmatically, i.e. she includes within that membership all who appear in her judgment to be confessing the same Lord Jesus Christ and to be responding to his love with love to their fellows, all, in short, who, because they recognize their common faith and life, find they can work together as a community.[4] In terms of this pragmatic definition the church of course must exercise discipline, excluding from her membership those who, because of their different understanding of God's love and of the church's work, find they cannot co-operate actively in her program but serve rather to obstruct or block her work. This matter of discipline is of course very difficult, for how does one exclude persons out of love for them? And yet, when it is remembered that all acts of the empirical church are pragmatic acts with no claims to final or ultimate justification, but simply the best human judgment to which the community can come in the light of its own understanding of its work in the world, the harsh and brittle edge so often apparent in church discipline will perhaps be somewhat tempered. If the empirical church claimed to be the eschatological community, and her binding and loosing here on earth were believed valid for heaven above and all eternity (cf. Matt. 16:19; 18:18), then it would be a different matter. But as long as the church remembers her empirical character and recognizes her own

[4] Cf. Karl Barth, *Church Dogmatics* (Edinburgh: T. and T. Clark, 1936-   ) I, 1, pp. 33 ff.

judgments as pragmatic and relative, she will realize there are other communities on earth through which God is also working, however difficult it may be for us to discern his work in those that differ radically from our understanding of the church's nature and mission. And it may well be that those, whom our church finds she must exclude to carry on her work, will find their proper task in God's kingdom within some other historical community.

It should be clear from this that just as the church's self-definition is pragmatic, so is her conception of "the world." For the conception of the world is relative to and polar with the conception of the church. The world is nothing but that place to which the church has been called to minister with God's love. The world consists of those who, as the empirical church sees it, are not yet consciously responding to God's gift in Jesus Christ and to whom, therefore, the church must witness. The world consists of those who, from the empirical church's vantage point, are not yet clear vehicles of God's forgiveness and redemption, and whom, therefore, the church must love and serve and forgive. In short, the world is nothing else than that place of real human need, as the empirical church sees it, to which the church finds she must give herself in response to God's love given for her need.

The conception of the world arises, then, because as the church proceeds in her work she finds some whose viewpoint and understanding, judgments and actions, seem so strange that she cannot effectively co-operate with them in bringing God's love and forgiveness to men. Perhaps these others with these strange ways call themselves Russian Communists, or Roman Catholics, or Southern Baptists, or Rotarians—their name matters not. Whoever they are, they are those with whom, in our limitations, we find we cannot effectively do what we understand to be our God-given task; indeed, we may find it necessary to oppose them vigorously. For us they are the "world," pragmatically defined in terms of the concrete action which love seems to us to require. Whenever we think this distinction between church and world, between "us" and "them," is more than pragmatic, and that we are somehow *better* than they, we are no longer acknowledging that we live simply by God's gracious forgiveness; on the contrary, we are boasting of our own virtue and have thereby become, in our spiritual pride, worse than they.

Despite all the difficulties in the distinction between church and world, it is one which we must make, for God's love is always mediated to us through some empirical community, and we in turn cannot respond to that love without taking up our task of service within some empirical community. To be human is therefore to live and work in terms of some such distinctions. Let us be careful not to confuse these empirical distinctions with those final distinctions holding for the eschaton; these God alone can make. The wheat cannot with certainty be distinguished from the tares until the time of the harvest (Matt. 13:24-30).

VI

We can now briefly tie together the various strands of this chapter. We have seen that the church is that community which remembers Jesus Christ and expects the coming kingdom of God; or, to say the same thing in another way, which lives in conscious response to God's purpose which—all historical evidence to the contrary notwithstanding—will ultimately prevail. At the same time, precisely because the church recognizes that the eschaton has not yet come and that she lives in the midst of the relativities of history, the church knows herself as empirical and limited with her conceptions and decisions pragmatically shaped. She knows, therefore, that she must exercise discipline, but she knows also that her judgments cannot be final. She knows that she must seek out the needs of the world and there serve, but she knows that her understanding of the world is limited and inadequate. The empirical church is thus the effective sociological unit within which Christian decisions and actions occur. The polar realities of church and world constitute the actual sociological context (theologically defined) within which Christian deciding, purposing, acting, and working proceed from day to day and year to year. Hence, only through analyzing and interpreting the empirical situation in terms of this concept of church-and-world, will our political, economic, social, and other decisions and work be seen in their theological import, i.e., in terms of the relevance to them of the redemption of human history by God's love.

4 The Individual Disciple

> "For freedom Christ has set us free; stand fast therefore, and do not submit again to a yoke of slavery. . . . For you were called to freedom, brethren; only do not use your freedom as an opportunity for the flesh, but through love be servants of one another. For the whole law is fulfilled in one word, 'You shall love your neighbor as yourself.'" (Gal. 5:1, 13-14)

WE HAVE SEEN THAT FOR THE CHRISTIAN RIGHT MORAL action must be understood as responsive to God's prior redemptive activity of love toward us and occurring within a context defined by the polar relation of church and world. Decisions and acts are never simply those of isolated individuals. For individuals are always members of a variety of communities—family, town, school, labor union, business community, and so forth—and it is as members of these communities that they decide and act. Cutting across the lines of these communities is the distinction between church and world—the church being that community that knows herself as the growing edge, as it were, of God's grace and love moving into the communities of the secular world to transform them into the kingdom of God. For any serious Christian—that is, for anyone seriously concerned to respond to God's sovereign rule in human history—the life and work of the church, as the living agent of God's love in human history, will be of the first importance. Decisions will be made in terms of the tension between church and world which grows out of the imperative laid upon the church to "make disciples of all nations" (Matt. 28:19).

Given this general context, we are ready to turn to the problem of the individual who must continuously make decisions. First we must analyze what decisions are and how they are related both to the individual and to the communities in which he stands.

I

We can understand the nature of decisions and actions with the aid of the concept *purpose*. A *decision* is the inward activity through which we set before ourselves a purpose to realize some goal in the near or distant future. An *action* is then the operation performed to carry out this purpose and bring into existence our objective. Now the important thing to note here is that all of these words—purpose, decision, action—can be understood only by regarding man as a "time-binding" animal,[1] one who is able to bind into a unity what would otherwise be isolated moments. To take an example: I set myself the purpose of getting a college education. When I make this decision, what I am really doing is resolving to tie together the next four years of my life in a unity of action. Since my objective

[1] The term "time-binding" (though not necessarily my particular usage) is Alfred Korzybski's. See *Manhood of Humanity* (New York: Dutton, 1921).

cannot be realized without four years of academic work, it lies in the relatively distant future. Moreover, it is something that does not now exist, and which will not exist, unless I bring it into being through my activity. Thus, a decision is always, on the one hand, the resolution to *bind together* that segment of future time required to realize the purpose under consideration; on the other hand, it is the resolve to *create* a reality, to bring into being something which does not now exist—in this case a college education for myself. It is clear that when we speak of decision we are speaking of a great and mysterious power of man, the power in the present to unify under a single purpose undetermined and unknown moments, days, and years of the future. Our ability to decide is our power over the future. Our *purpose* is the particular shape we intend to give that future. In this case, the next four years are to be spent studying, rather than, for example, clerking in the local grocery store.

A human life is a complex ordering and patterning of purposes related to each other in very complicated ways. Some purposes are related directly to specific biological needs, e.g., for food, shelter, sexual gratification. Others derive from our aesthetic sensitivities, our awareness of ethical demands, our intellectual interests, and the like. Many interests and needs are of course involved whenever we make a choice such as to enter college. But the important thing to note is that this new decision brings a certain ordering into the structure of purposes in which we are living. When we make the choice, in effect we resolve to order our interests for the next four years in accordance with the demands of this particular purpose. Not that we no longer will need or desire food, or pleasure, or other nonacademic goods. Rather, we have set ourselves to achieving these other objectives only within the context of this major goal.

Thus, I will not, for example, take a full-time job which might give me an income making possible more exotic meals and more pleasant and relaxed evening hours. These desires, however necessary, will be put in a subordinate place so that I can devote considerable time to study. When particular small decisions are called for, they will be made (perhaps almost unconsciously) in terms of my overarching purpose. Thus, if I must decide whether to study tonight for tomorrow's examination, or go to a movie and relax, a significant factor working in this decision will be my long-range intention to obtain a college degree. This does not necessarily mean I will choose to study; it may be that I will decide to take the evening off. But the minor decision will be made with consideration for the long-range objective. If not, if it is made without reference to this supposed objective, one could legitimately ask whether the decision to obtain a college education has been seriously taken—or whether, perhaps, the really effective decision has been to gain such pleasure as I can from one day to the next.

This analysis, of course, has been greatly oversimplified. In actual fact all of us have a number of overarching purposes under which there are sub-purposes and sub-sub-purposes. Thus, my decision to get a college education will itself be made in terms of other purposes, e.g., to become a doctor. Since I cannot become a doctor without first getting an education, I decide to devote the next several years of my life to realizing the condition necessary to achievement of the more distant goal. However, I cannot get a college education without paying for it, so I may decide to accept certain kinds of summer employment to earn money for tuition. The relatively unimportant immediate decision about attending the movie tonight may be made in terms of any or all of these larger overarching purposes by which I am ordering my life.

But this image of an ordered hierarchy of purposes still oversimplifies and falsifies the actual situation. For it is often the case that major decisions grow out of minor ones, and sometimes we alter the leading purposes that have been guiding our choices for years. Thus, while in college, I may, in order to fulfill some class assignment in, e.g., history, do some reading that introduces me to the interesting possibilities of politics, and this may lead me to a change of plans from a medical career to that of politician. None of our purposes, however important and final they may seem at the moment they are made, are irrevocable. Unforeseen circumstances may always arise leading us to see things in a different light and thus change our plans in some slight or some far-reaching way. Far from being fixed and final, our purposes are the living structures of the current postures of our beings, the orientations which our selves have at this particular moment. But precisely because this orientation or posture is a living structure, not a dead one, it is sensitive to what occurs round about it and can respond creatively to every new situation. It is just this sensitive and responsive living structure of purposes which our word *self* denotes.

We must now relate what we have been saying here to our earlier discussion about the relation of selves to the histories and communities in which they find themselves. We have been sketching the purposes of the individual as related to his own decisions. But this individual, with his private purposes, is an abstraction. For no individual is isolated from others in such a way that his purposes are his alone. Thus, the child does not go to school simply on his own initiative; he attends because of certain decisions his parents have made. But even this statement vastly over-simplifies. The parents' choices in this matter are affected by compulsory education laws (i.e., by decisions made in legislatures and elsewhere), and by the character of the public, in comparison with the private, schools in their community. Thus, the decisions of school boards, deter-mining policy for the public schools, are also involved, as are the choices of the voters who elected the board mem-bers. And so on and on. One could carry the matter back through the history of education—indeed, of culture as a whole—each earlier decision playing its important and unique role in the matter of the child's attending school. This, of course, is only one example. All other decisions of the individual are similarly involved with, and in-fluenced by, prior decisions and purposes of many other individuals and communities, going as far back in history as one chooses. The overarching purposes, in terms of which our day-by-day decisions are made, are not merely our own purposes (as the earlier discussion perhaps sug-gested); included also are purposes of individuals and com-munities quite unknown to us but nonetheless effectively working within our decisions.

II

We are now in a position to deal briefly with a problem that has vexed much ethical discussion, the problem of free-dom and determinism. It should be clear from what has been said that any sort of absolute freedom for every al-ternative in each moment is meaningless and impossible. But it should also be clear that the self cannot be properly described in terms of some mechanistic or deterministic scheme. We can see why both of these positions must be rejected if we note more closely what has already been discovered about the nature of freedom. Freedom is the power to *bind time*. It is the power of a self at one moment to tie together succeeding moments and even years by means of an overarching purpose. If I could not do this, clearly I would not be free. For what else could a free decision be than the power to govern subsequent actions in terms of the goal I have set myself?

But if freedom is thus the power to bind time, then future time must actually be *bound* in some way not true before my free decision. To return to our example, having once decided to attend college, I do not reopen the question in every moment of the subsequent four years. That question I allow to remain more or less closed, and other decisions are made accordingly. Of course, it is always possible for me to reconsider and conclude, perhaps, that college is not for me, but ordinarily I refrain from this unless some unforeseen crisis arises calling into question the wisdom of the earlier choice. Ordinarily, I allow my course of action to be *determined* by the earlier decision, and my present decisions are made within the context of that previous one. That is, I allow myself to be *bound* with respect to the earlier choice. Thus the *past* decision determines my present action. In this respect I am determined by the past.

Moreover, apart from such determination by the past I could not be free. For if my decisions in the past did not really conclude something, thus actually beginning to shape my future, to speak of them as free would be meaningless. It is precisely in his power to bind his future that man is free. Freedom then, is an empty word unless we acknowledge that the future in fact is determined in some significant fashion by earlier choices.

Furthermore, it is clear that each of us, if he really is free, has the power to bind others. The decisions of the parent about the child's attendance at school must in fact effectively bind the child, else the parent has no freedom with respect to his child. My words must actually influence you in some way, or to speak of my freedom with reference to you is absurd. But the converse of this is, of course, that the child in fact is bound in some measure by the parent's decisions, and you are really influenced by my words.

Thus, to speak of ourselves as determined by our past decisions and by the decisions of others—by our individual histories and by the histories of the communities to which we belong going all the way back to the beginning—is not to speak of some kind of mechanical determinism. On the contrary, it is to apprehend the way selves are free, viz., in their power to bind time. It is to understand that a self is that very complicated kind of reality, the structure of which is formed by the decisions and purposes of the past, but which has the power effectively to bind the future through free decisions in the present. On the one hand, freedom means my power to bind time, i.e, to affect the future by my present decision; but if time is really bound by free choices, then my present has its character because of past decisions no longer in my control. On the other hand, if past decisions and actions have in fact determined the present situation, then selves evidently must have the power effectively and freely to shape their futures. The determination of our present situation by the past is not, then, mechanical, or rigid. Rather, it is such as to provide the context of meaning and purpose necessary for the existence of a free self which in this present moment must decide about the future.

This complex structure of freedom and determination can be illuminated by two simple examples. When a man decides to become a pianist, he at once binds himself and begins to free himself. He binds himself to practicing several hours a day, year in and year out for the unforeseeable future. This involves a real determination of the future. But precisely because of this binding, as this future unfolds, the man becomes progressively freer: his proficiency on the keyboard grows until he can play Bach or Bartok at will, and he thus gains a freedom which he did not have before. Freedom and determination by the past are not mutually exclusive; they are involved in each other and mutually require each other.

The same point can be made with reference to dialogue or conversation. When one person asks another a question, it is clear that his words significantly determine the other's rejoinder. That is, the other, if this is indeed a conversation, will reply *to the question asked*, he will speak relevantly to the issue. This is possible only if his consciousness and his speech have been effectively influenced by the prior speech of the other. But it would be ridiculous to say that his reply has therefore been, in some mechanical or logical way, determined by the other. On the contrary, only if he answers the other's query *freely* is it truly a reply. The first person asks the question precisely because he does not know the answer, because the answer cannot be mechanically or logically derived from the question. The rejoinder, then, will be in some sense a free and unpredictable and unexpected response. And yet if it is an answer to just this question and not some other, it will be relevant to and significantly determined by the question asked. For it is of the very essence of dialogue that one be affected by the other significantly and yet be responding spontaneously to what the other has said. Without allowing for the presence of both these elements—determination by the other together with real freedom and spontaneity and creativity in the self—it is not possible to understand what actually occurs whenever we converse. This means, once again, that freedom of the self and determination by the other are not mutually exclusive, but are in fact interdependent, neither being possible without the other.

The self, then, we must say in summary, is that exceedingly complex reality which is always free and spontaneous and creative in the present moment precisely because it lives out of, and is in some significant way bound by, the decisions and actions of itself and other selves in the past. A self is a structure—a structure of purposes—but it is a living structure of living purposes, and thus it is a structure with the power of freedom.

III

We are now in a position to return to the analysis of the moral situation of the individual Christian. It should now be clear that it is superficial and irrelevant to discuss Christian ethics simply in terms of rules of conduct the individual is to follow in making his decisions. For the really important consideration here is the structure of purposes—i.e., the *character* of the individual—in terms of which all his decisions are made. Christian ethics must have something to do with this living structure or it has little to do with the real self. It is this structure which in fact makes such decisions as are made. The concern of the Christian moralist, then, must be with the development of self-structures which are capable of deciding in accordance with the demands of the Christian gospel. It is not enough simply to lay down those demands heteronomously, expecting them to be obeyed. Such moral exhortation is both superficial and irresponsible. Moreover, such a position is basically that of the law, which, as Paul rightly saw, is transcended in the Christian view. The Christian gospel is not concerned with keeping this or that law or principle regarded as somehow the very command of God; that way lies Judaism. On the contrary, it is for "freedom [that] Christ has set us free; [we must] stand fast therefore, and . . . not submit again to a yoke of slavery" (Gal. 5:1).

What now is the relation of this Christian freedom of which Paul speaks to that freedom which is at the very heart of the structure of the self? I think we can say they are identical, though not in a way that is immediately evident. Paul is speaking of the true fulfillment of human existence: to be truly a man is to be free; it is to be one who lives in spontaneous and creative relations with other selves; it is to be one who loves. But in our analysis of the self, we too have seen this to be the case. For a true self is one who is free to respond to other selves in conversation and free to shape his own destiny within a community, that is, in response to and rapport with the decisions and purposes of those round about him.

Does this mean, then, that all selves are Christian selves, and all lives are Christian? Not at all. In our earlier analysis we explored the nature of selfhood as a structure of interlaced decisions and purposes. But we did not analyze the way in which particular kinds of decisions tend to weaken this very structure, while others strengthen it. We did not ask whether particular kinds of purposes may effectively inhibit and even destroy freedom, while others open it up. It is to these questions that ethics proper is directed. Hence, we must turn now to a consideration of the distinction between the healthy and the diseased self, the self which is whole and saved in contrast with the self which is broken and lost, the self that is truly free in contrast with the self in bondage to sin.

It should be clear in the first place that the notions of bondage and freedom make sense only in terms of some such conception of the self as we have here developed. As Augustine long ago saw, it is only a *free* being that can be described meaningfully as "bound," its freedom in some way being inhibited or restricted. And it is only a free being become bound that can be described meaningfully as having been "set free." A stick or a stone—a thing—is never "set free." To give it freedom would be to transform it into something else than a thing, namely, a person. It is only a person, whose basic nature is freedom—but whose freedom has become radically restricted—that can be described as "set free." When Paul, therefore, speaks of Christ setting us free, he is speaking of Christ enabling us to come into our own from a situation in which we were not fully what we were intended to be, free men.

We need not discuss here again the way in which God's action of love and forgiveness, manifested to man in Jesus Christ two thousand years ago, is communicated in wider and wider historical circles through the preaching and life of the church. Nor need we repeat again that the church lives and works in the hope that this love of God, now known only as foretaste, will ultimately engulf all of human history and existence. But it is important that we indicate here the meaning of all this for the fulfillment of the individual, how it makes possible his emergence as a free self. It is the Christian claim—and this should be intelligible in terms of the interpretation of selfhood we have been developing—that truly free selves can develop only within the context of a community of love, or, better put, only within the kingdom of God.

If the paradigm of true freedom is conversation or dialogue, it should not be too difficult to see why this is so. In order for a dialogue to take place two things are necessary, that I *understand* what the other is saying, and that I have *sufficient security* in his presence to respond freely and honestly. If there were no understanding, obviously there could be no conversation for it would not be possible for one person to respond relevantly to the other's words. Meaningful and significant dialogue becomes increasingly a possibility only as real understanding develops. But again, even if I understood the other, but feared to respond with truth because I knew he would be offended and resentful, there could be no real dialogue. Instead would occur the artificial, dishonest conversations in which we all engage, conversations that conceal the truth from the other as much as reveal it. Only if we could have confidence that false and destructive responses on our part would be forgiven by the other—that there would be sufficient strength in the communal ties between us to sustain our relationship in the face of the rupture genuinely honest rejoinders might effect—could we really be free in our responses. Freedom becomes possible, then, only when the community in which I exercise my decisions is sufficiently vital and strong both to make possible real understanding between those conversing and to give sufficient security for the participating selves to risk speaking and acting spontaneously and openly.

In none of our empirical communities are these conditions fully met, and precisely for this reason none of us is

genuinely free in his relations to others. We fail to understand each other and so we distrust each other and respond
in inappropriate ways. And then our ill responses and our
distrust lead us into further misunderstandings. Further,
because we distrust and fear our companions, we are un-
willing to reveal ourselves to each other, creatively and
openly disclosing ourselves. Instead we conceal ourselves
with masks both from others and from ourselves. These
conditions which make us stunted and unfree are found
in every family, every relationship between friends, every
community. They force us to live in bondage to hatred and
fear, to anxiety and distrust. We are not the free selves who
can creatively bind time; on the contrary, we are ourselves
bound by the network of guilt and despair and sin in
which we are immersed.

In contrast with this, consider an authentic community
of love. Here would be a continuous seeking to understand
the other together with a fundamental rapport that would
make possible appreciating what the other is saying and
doing. Moreover, here would be genuine security in relations to others so one could take the risk of freely and
openly being oneself, speaking one's mind, acting creatively. For one could be confident that the others would not
betray or stab in the back if the action proved wrong; on
the contrary, they would have the strength to absorb the
destructive effects of the sinful act and could thus forgive.
Here, then, would be a community in which real dialogue
could occur. Here would be a situation in which one could
dare to make radically creative decisions affecting the future of himself and others. For here one could have the
confidence that these decisions would never finally destroy
what was cherished and valued within the community—however wrong they turned out to be—because the community

of love was willing and able to accept the risk of the freedom of its members.

It should be clear that as long as selves live isolated and alone, alienated from themselves and separated from each other, they cannot become the free beings they sometimes begin to become when they love each other. Moreover, only if the all-embracing community, inclusive of all the sub-communities in which we live and act, were a community of love, would such real freedom become possible. The connection of this with the Christian faith ought now to be obvious. For the Christian gospel is the proclamation that God himself is at work in his world, transforming it into just such a community as this. That is, according to the Christian claim the ultimate reality in the universe—God— is personal and loving. Since this is the *ultimate* reality with which we have to do, there is here a basis for real conviction that the community of which the gospel speaks will not be destroyed. This is, therefore, a community in which we can take the risk of acting freely, spontaneously, creatively, even though this community has not yet been fully established. It is in the community that knows God's love and forgiveness, and seeks to respond to it through forgiveness and love of both friends and enemies that real freedom begins to be a possibility for human existence. It is thus in the church—insofar as the church is that empirical community which lives by its anticipation and expectation and devotion to the coming eschatological community of love, the kingdom of God—that we become responsive and responsible selves. As we take up our crosses within this community, and become Christ's disciples who genuinely give themselves in love, we become free persons.

Of course it is not easy for us to appropriate this freedom for which Christ has set us free. For the community of love within which we can begin to live responsively and creatively is not simply the empirical church which is clearly visible here and now. Rather, it is the eschatological community known to our hope and faith. The available empirical evidence for the most part undermines belief in the reality of this community and in the possibility of this authentic freedom. For the empirical evidence around us, even in the church itself, points to distrust, hatred, fear, anxiety and war, not love. It is on the basis of our faith in God, then, and only on that basis, that we can act with real freedom even in the church. But if we have faith, we can and do become free men who shape their own destinies, create their own futures.

It is in this context that Paul's admonition in Philippians becomes clear. Listen to what he says: "work out your own salvation with fear and trembling; for God is at work in you, both to will and to work for his good pleasure" (2:12-13). In this paradoxical verse Paul has expressed precisely the point we have here been making. It is because God is at work in us that we can and must work out our own salvation. It is because he comes to us in real love, and genuine love creates free beings who can respond to it, that we are now enabled to live and act in freedom. We could not work out our salvation if we had not been freed, that is, if God were not at work within us establishing us in our freedom. But God's saving work is precisely his setting us free, enabling us to become beings who can decide and act out of their own creativity. Such freedom will, of course, always be appropriated in "fear and trembling," as Paul has it here, for it will be based on faith, not clear knowledge, on hope, not present certainties. And being real freedom, it will be the source of possibly serious mistakes and blunders that may injure us and others. It will be, then, with "fear and trembling" that we will act in our freedom, but we will be able to act freely nonetheless if we believe that God himself is actually at work within us, both to will and to work according to his loving purposes.

IV

We must tie these threads together in terms of the problems of Christian ethics. It is now clear that the problem of the individual, for Christian ethics, is the problem of living as a free man in a hoped-for community of love. No codes or laws of right and wrong, no rules defining moral behavior, no moral principles or ethical ideals will be able to resolve the ethical problem of the individual. For serious dependence on any such involves the attempt to escape from the requirement that in each new moment we decide freely and act. It thus leads to rejection of God's salvation and disobedience to his will as well as to the destruction of our own personal existence. Our task is not to obey this or that rule in regard to smoking or drinking or going to war. Our task is to be free persons in God's kingdom, responding freely to his love for us, giving ourselves freely in love to neighbors and enemies, participating creatively in God's creative work. There are no rules or principles that tell us how to be free and creative; all such rules and principles are "law" in the Pauline sense, the law which Christ has abolished. We must be willing to take the risk of living creatively and freely in the midst of the communities in which we find ourselves, responding not legally but with love, meeting each moment with openness, daring to act in accordance with the demands of each new situation upon our love—which is to say, we must be willing to live open to God's will for us in each situation.

This life obviously will be lived in "fear and trembling." It will be a life misunderstood by many, perhaps resulting in our own historical destruction. But it is the only life the Christian dare live. If we once get clear the radicalness of the gospel's claim that we are called to be free men within a community of love, together with the radicalness of the gospel's demand that the church be the cutting edge of God's transformation of hatred and sin into the kingdom of his love, then we can at last consider the very practical question with which ethics is concerned, the question of decision between right and wrong. To analysis of this question we will turn in the next chapter.

5 The Problem of Decision

"You have heard that it was said, 'You shall love your neighbor and hate your enemy.' But I say to you, Love your enemies and pray for those who persecute you, so that you may be sons of your Father who is in heaven." (Matt. 5:43-45)

WE HAVE BEEN TRYING IN THESE CHAPTERS TO OUTLINE THE perspective of the Christian ethic. Its principal characteristic, sharply distinguishing it from naturalistic and humanistic ethics, is its grounding in the standpoint of Christian faith. Christian faith, in turn, understands itself as rooted in the loving action of the God who has created the world and who has brought into being in the course of history a community which knows his love and seeks to respond to it, thus becoming its vehicle in human affairs. God's ultimate purpose for history is the creation of his kingdom—the community of perfect love within which individuals can become truly free and creative, fulfilling God's original purposes for man.

Already the church knows—as a kind of foretaste of the

kingdom—something of the quality of love and the possibilities of real freedom and creativity for which she believes man is destined. Her hope and expectation that
God will make these anticipations the very substance of
human existence make possible such loving self-sacrifice,
and freedom from legal codes and other idolatries, as
she knows in her present existence. It is in this hope
that the church lives in those moments when she actually
becomes the community destined finally to be the kingdom
of God. And it is in this hope that individuals within the
church live in those moments when they become genuinely
free spirits, able to give themselves in love to friends and
enemies alike. In this sense the Christian hope, itself rooted
in the Christian faith, is the essential ground and basis for
all Christian deciding and acting: the Christian ethic is an
eschatological ethic.

We must in this concluding chapter attempt to see what
these observations mean for the practical day-to-day decisions with which Christian individual and community are
faced. However, it must be emphasized that in turning now
to so-called practical problems we will not be resolving
the moral dilemma. We have seen that the Christian life is
above all a free life, one in which each takes upon himself
the responsibility before God for his own decisions. There
can, therefore, be no final answers to any genuine moral
problems; indeed, there cannot even be settled questions.
Only for perspectives other than faith in the living God
can issues be settled in advance. For a faith that understands it must ever be responsive to God's love in accordance
with the unique character of each historical situation, it is
never possible to lay down rules. One can only live in continuous receptiveness to the will of God and living responsiveness to every need of the neighbor, and then

freely and creatively decide in each moment to do what appears required of love for that moment, always taking responsibility for one's action. With this forewarning, that we will be unable to settle any "practical" questions in advance because such questions can be settled, as the word suggests, only in *practice*, that is, in *actual decision and action*, we proceed to an analysis of the problem of deciding and acting.

I

The Christian of course (whether individual or community) does not come to this matter of practical action *de novo*. If the analysis of the previous chapters has been correct, it will be clear that every decision occurs within the context of an ongoing historical process. One comes to every new decision having made previous decisions which have shaped one's character in certain ways and have obligated one to others in various ways. One always comes as a person with previous commitments, to family, to friends, to nation, to church, to many other communities—to God. And it is in terms of these commitments that the present decision must inevitably be made. This means that every decision will be complex and difficult. For failure to honor one's prior obligations is to break faith with other persons, to disrupt community with them. Though this may be necessary on occasion, it is difficult to justify from the point of view of an ethic whose primary concern is the building of real community among men. Moreover, the diversity of commitments in which different individuals and communities are involved will necessarily mean that what is "right" for one individual or group may not be right for some other. It may well be right for a surgeon in certain circumstances to open a man's chest and operate on his heart; it is doubtful if it would ever be right for me to do so. The situation in which one stands, one's own aptitudes and prior commitments, the freedom of the Christian man before God, and the adaptability of love itself to every possible situation, all mean that Christian decisions can never be governed by inflexible rules.

But from this it does not follow that no principles or guides for decision-making can be suggested. Indeed, such a position would reduce the Christian ethic to practical acceptance of the *status quo*, when in fact it involves radical rejection of every *status quo* in favor of the demands of the kingdom of God. How, then, do the demands of the kingdom impinge upon us in concrete terms? What concrete demands are laid upon me in my every moment of decision? The general answer to these questions, of course, is that I am required to give myself without reservation to neighbor and enemy alike in love. But our question is: What now, in my actual moments of choice, does love require me to do?

It should be clear from the previous chapters that this is not something to be answered simply on the basis of our vague intuitions or definite conceptions of love; it is to be answered, so far as possible, in terms of God's revelation to us of what love is and requires. "In this is love," writes the author of the first letter of John, "not that we loved God but that he loved us and sent his Son to be the expiation for our sins" (4:10). The model of love in terms of which we must reach our decisions is God's act of self-giving in Jesus Christ. If we take seriously the notion that God has here revealed himself and his will, it will be this alone which we will seek to make determinative of our decisions. Although in our continuous failure to obey his will other factors drawn from our sinful selves and situations will also become effectual, our conscious effort must ever be directed toward deciding and acting solely in terms of the obligations laid on us in God's revelation. To take any position other than this would be to deny either that God has actually revealed his will for us, or that it is in fact God—the creator of our being and Lord of our destiny—whose will has been made known.

II

If God's action in Jesus Christ is the true paradigm of loving action, there are several things clearly implied. In the first place, it is evident that self-interest has no part to play in Christian action. It is because "God so loved the *world* that he gave his only Son" (John 3:16). This love made known in God's revelation is always concerned for the other, never for the self. Hence, Christian action never worries about self-preservation. This is the absurdity of the Christian ethic: it is an ethic of radical imprudence. One must be willing to deny oneself absolutely for the sake of the neighbor. Clearly this means more than sacrificing a few pleasures; it means willingness to give up everything that we cherish as goods—perhaps our friends, our ideals, our way of life, perhaps even our personal virtue and hope for heavenly reward. Paul saw clearly that the Christian must even be prepared willingly to accept damnation if that should serve the neighbor's need. If it would be of any avail for the "sake of my brethren, my kinsmen by race," he said, "I could wish that I myself were accursed and cut off from Christ" (Rom. 9:3). The first conclusion suggested by God's revelation, then, is that Christian action must always be focused on the need of the other, not the self.

This leads directly to the second thing to be said, namely, that Christian action must always be directed to the situations where need is greatest. Wherever suffering is, there the Christian must go. But he must make particular efforts to enter situations characterized by sinful rebellion against God and absence of love for fellows. Christ came to heal the sick and wounded, but he also came to save sinners: in sin, human suffering of soul reaches its peak. Hence, no Christian has the right to avoid "dirty" situations which might soil his hands or wound his person. If it is thought that politics or war are sinful and evil situations, it is precisely there that the Christian is required to go with his ministry of reconciliation. For the Christian must be one who, like his Master, is called the very friend of sinners (cf. Matt. 11:19; Luke 7:34).

Love, in sharp contrast with every other conception of goodness, is concerned to relate itself especially to its enemies, to sinners. Love exists only in such relationships. God's love for man is evident, not in God's loving man in response to man's love for God, but in God's actively reconciling man to himself while man was in enmity and rebellion against him (Rom. 5:10, I John 4:10, 19, and *passim*). The Christian is not required simply to love those who love him and are members of the "beloved community"; even the publicans and the Gentiles do that (Matt. 5:46-47). Christian love as perfectly exemplified in God's act in Christ sacrifices itself for and to sin; Christian love gives itself to its own enemies. This self-sacrifice to the evils of the sinful situation is so radical and complete that Paul finds it necessary to say that in its perfect expression, Christ "who knew no sin" was made "to be sin . . . so that in him we might become the righteousness of God" (II Cor. 5:21). Love goes to the very heart of the most sinful situations that it can find and there it gives of itself without reservation.[1]

This movement of love into the worst human conditions means that there is never justification for the Christian to give up any situation as lost beyond redemption. For this would imply that sometimes things are bad enough to warrant doing nothing. But as we have seen, the needier the situation, the greater the demand on love to enter and work redemptively. Again God's love must be our model. God does not forsake man even when man decides against him and pursues a sinful and disobedient course. The whole Old Testament is the story of God's faithfulness with Israel through all manner of betrayals. Finally, when Israel seems beyond hope, instead of giving up his efforts, God in his love goes beyond anything he has done before and sacrifices of himself. *Agape* is just that which is never stopped by rebuffs: the more impossible the situation, the more

[1] The Anabaptist-Mennonite tradition has always tried to interpret love in the radical sense of the New Testament, but in its tendency to withdraw from participation in the power struggles of the world it has badly compromised itself. On the Mennonite view, it is just in the power struggles, where self-centered individuals and groups attempt to dominate others, that are found both the essence and the most terrible expression of sin. For this reason Mennonites have felt unable to participate in these struggles. And yet, it is the character of love, not that it retreats from its opposite, but that it rushes in to act redemptively. The tendency in the Anabaptist-Mennonite tradition has been to see clearly one side of this paradox and to neglect the other. And from this has followed the conviction that we have a right—nay, even a duty—to withdraw from certain aspects of human life and society simply because we think those aspects are sinful. But this is failing to love just as certainly as is action out of the sinful desire to dominate. In sharp opposition to any strategy of withdrawal—which is usually motivated by the kind of love known to the publicans and Gentiles—Christian love always takes *responsibility* for the sinful situation.

effort it makes to redeem the offender. "Love bears all things, believes all things, hopes all things, endures all things. Love never ends." (I Cor. 13:7-8.)

If the situation appears hopeless, we must remember that we act and live finally in our hope that *God* will bring in his kingdom, not in the expectation that our own accomplishments will be great. Though it may appear impossible that any good could come of our persistence in loving where no response is forthcoming, "all things are possible with God" (Mark 10:27). The Christian, then, is one who gives up everything he possesses, and himself as well, not merely for people who are "good" and might seem to deserve such sacrifice, nor even for people on the "borderline" in whom we see possibilities of real transformation, but for the worst sinners, those for whom there seems no hope at all.

In the third place, if God's love is our model, we must say that love is that which is directed to persons as persons, that is, that the Christian life is a ministry of reconciliation. It is a healing of personal wounds, a restoring of that which destroys personal existence. We have in the preceding chapters described the nature of personal existence in both its social and individual dimensions, and neither can be omitted here for they are two sides of the same thing. We will not be able to neglect men in their social relations, for as we have seen, in large part their social relations determine the kind of individuals they are. But neither will we be able to neglect them in their uniqueness and individuality, for there can be no community of love that does not consist of free, creative, spontaneous individuals. We must, then, work toward transforming the communities in which we and other men stand into true communities of love—that is, into the kingdom of God—and simultaneously work toward the freeing of individuals from every kind of bondage for genuine creativity and openness before God.

Christian love, we can say in summary, always seeks to act both creatively and redemptively with and for persons imprisoned in sin and suffering, and this it does with eye exclusively on the need of the other, with no concern for the needs of the self. This is what is required of every Christian individual and community whenever called to make a decision—which is to say, in every moment.

III

But this still does not tell us what we ought to do in the concrete choices each of us face every moment. Were there only two people in the world, myself and another, it would go a long way toward giving such guidance. For in that situation the principal moral question would be: How can I serve the other's true interests most effectively? Even these decisions would not always be easy, for in our finite ignorance we seldom know precisely what kind of response the other needs from us. Few parents, for example, know when and precisely how they ought to punish their child so as not to injure or embitter his personality but help him grow into a creative and loving person.

But, however simple or difficult these questions might be in a world of two persons, it is obvious they become almost infinitely complicated merely by introducing a third. Such a change means far more than a mere doubling of the problems. Now a whole new order of problems is introduced: How am I to divide my time and efforts between these two confronting me? Each has different needs and different capacities; how do I allow for this? To take an extreme example, were one an idiot and the other a genius, I obviously would have to act in very different ways toward each, giving one what I denied the other. But by what principle could these decisions be made? Doubtless my efforts to build community among ourselves would meet with diverse responses from these differing individuals. But what could be done about this? Should I give greater time and attention to the one who is more responsive, or to the other? It seems I ought to respond to the former's love with a fuller giving of myself to him; but on the other hand, it is apparently the unresponsive one who actually needs my love the more.

In some situations I might have to choose between my two friends. To take an extreme case again—but one critical for the problem of Christian nonresistance—I might one day come upon the one in the act of shooting the other. What should I do now? If I myself shoot Cain, who has gun in hand, I destroy all possibilities of further giving myself in love to him; if I do not, he will shoot Abel, and then I no longer can serve him. Since Cain is evidently more in need of redemptive love, perhaps I should refrain from shooting; but certainly this seems both unjust and unloving to Abel who has been responsive to my love with love of his own. What, then, does love require me to do?

It should be clear from this example that merely to say we should love absolutely does not resolve the problem of decision, even in a world consisting of only three persons. In the actual world of several billion, the problems of decision are multiplied beyond imagination. We are responsible, somehow, to meet human need anywhere and everywhere we find it; we are obligated to love everyone. How is it possible to make choices in this kind of situation? Clearly, to respond to God's will responsibly we need some principles of selection, enabling us to give preference to certain claims while rejecting others. For without such selection we could not act at all. It is on this issue that the widest disagreements among Christian moralists in the contemporary scene are to be found. Few responsible writers would question the absoluteness of the obligation to love laid on the Christian. Few would question that this obligation directs us into situations of sin and suffering. The disputed and unresolved issue concerns this matter of actual preference and selection in the concrete choices which we must make.

It is commonly held [2] that this problem can and should be resolved by reference to the standard of justice. Whereas love is appropriate and meaningful in personal face-to-face relations, justice, precisely because it is more abstract and general, is impartial and objective, and thus appropriate to large-scale social relations. Situations that require me to decide between the needs of several neighbors, therefore, should be dealt with in terms of justice. Although love, conceived as absolute self-giving, may be significant and relevant in close personal relations, when applied to the problems of the social order, it is at best an "impossible possibility." [3]

There is no time here to give this position the full analysis it deserves. I can only point out that introducing the category of justice does not, as is supposed, in any way lessen the problem of preferential decisions in a complex social order. For the problem simply reappears in the form

[2] See, e.g., Reinhold Niebuhr *Moral Man and Immoral Society* (New York: Scribners, 1932) and *Interpretation of Christian Ethics* (New York: Harper, 1935); E. Brunner, *Divine Imperative* (Philadelphia: Westminster Press, 1947) and *Justice and the Social Order* (New York: Harper, 1945); P. Ramsey, *Basic Christian Ethics* (New York: Scribners, 1950).

[3] See, e.g., Niebuhr, *Interpretation of Christian Ethics*, Ch. 4.

of the question: How can I be just to everyone every-where? How is it possible for me to deal impartially with every man when I do not and cannot have relations with more than a few? The principle of justice taken by itself is of no more help in the concrete problems of decision-making than is the command to love. If it has seemed so, that is be-cause its less radical character—allowing a place for the needs and desires of the self, along with the needs of the neighbor—makes justice appear a more feasible objective. But we have really only transposed the problem of con-crete decision-making not resolved it, to say nothing of the fact that in watering love down to the level of justice, we have tempered God's wisdom with our foolishness. We must, then, return to Christian love and ask if any princi-ples of preference arise immanently out of it.

IV

It appears to me that four considerations, deriving from the Christian revelation of God's love for us in our sin, can be isolated and significantly discussed in this context. Though neither separately nor collectively will they present us with *the* answer to any concrete problem of moral de-cision, each calls our attention to certain critical questions that should be considered in every decision. As will be seen, these considerations exist in a certain tension with each other, and this tension is never resolved except in the moment of decision itself.

One of these matters, justice, has already been mentioned. Though considerations of justice do not resolve the prob-lem of decision-making, they must enter into every de-cision for the sake of love itself. For love demands that I give myself to the needs of every man, not simply this one or that one. There is no one whom I have the right to exclude from my love. Not that I am required to deal with each in the same way; that would be unloving. The needs of men are different, and love must minister in accordance with need. But all men I confront have needs to which I can minister, and my ministrations cannot be governed by partiality and favoritism, but must be the expression of justice. This can be seen clearly in the family. The parents ought to love all the children in some sense equally. It would be unjust, and thus unloving, for them to play favorites, showering attention on one and ignoring another. The demand for justice here is a demand of love itself. But precisely because it is demanded by *love*, it is clear this can be no even-handed justice which gives precisely the same *thing* to every child. Rather, as love, it will seek to meet the unique and individual needs of each child.

From this demand for justice arising from love itself, *1* there derives a quasi-utilitarian principle which when explicitly formulated, can be a guide in making decisions. One ought to do whatever will serve to the highest degree the genuine needs of the greatest number of persons. On the surface, this principle may appear to be a concise expression of the implications for social ethics of the Christian imperative to love, and it has often been so interpreted. However, as we shall see, though one authentic strand of those implications is laid bare here, the matter is really far more complex than this simple formula suggests.

The requirement of justice in our loving is not the only one we must consider. A second consideration, of at least *2* equal importance, has to do with the special responsibilities belonging to every individual and every group. There are several sorts of special responsibilities that are relevant here. In the first place, I have responsibilities deriving from my particular aptitudes and talents. "Every one to whom much is given, of him will much be required." (Luke 12: 48.) If I have special musical aptitudes, I should not seek to serve my neighbor through digging ditches; if I am awkward with my hands, I should not seek to become a surgeon. One's peculiar talents and aptitudes open up special opportunities not accessible to others. In a community of love each should serve in accordance with his unique gifts. As Paul put it: "Now there are varieties of gifts, but the same Spirit; and there are varieties of service, but the same Lord; and there are varieties of working, but it is the same God who inspires them all in every one. To each is given the manifestation of the Spirit for the common good." (I Cor. 12:4-7.)

A second kind of special responsibilities devolves from the promises and commitments we have made. Promising is the act of binding the self to another for some future time. When I have promised to meet another at a particular time and place, I have laid on myself a special obligation to see that the meeting is kept. Moreover, this obligation takes a certain precedence over other responsibilities that might arise as I am on the road to the meeting place. Not that the obligation is absolute, so that I must "pass by on the other side" if I meet a man who has been beaten almost to death. But certainly love obliges me to keep the appointment if possible, lest I break faith with the other. Our lives are filled with special obligations rooted this way in commitments made to others and to ourselves. Some such obligations are trivial, but some are momentous, as with the promise to live one's entire life with another.

Closely related to the special responsibilities that are mine by virtue of my peculiar aptitudes or particular promises, are those that fall to me because of the roles I play in society. When I get married I take up a new role, the role of husband. In so doing I obligate myself not only to my wife to whom I promise responsible performance of the duties of this role, but also to society at large which defines for me and my wife what it is to be a husband in twentieth-century America—something quite different from, e.g., contemporary China, or ancient Israel. Of course one plays many roles simultaneously and with each go special responsibilities. As a father I have particular obligations to my own children which I do not have to others: I am charged in a special way with their care and upbringing. As a son I have particular obligations to my parents which I do not have with respect to other adults. As a teacher I have a special responsibility for my students which I do not have for everyone I meet on the street. If I were a doctor, I would have particular responsibilities to the sick; if a newspaper editor, to my readers; if a merchant, to those who bought from me. We always play definite roles in the various communities in which we participate, and these roles lay upon us special responsibilities which we are obligated to discharge.

The important point to note here is that these responsibilities must often be given priority in our decisions over the claims of the first consideration we mentioned, justice. It is clear that we do not and we ought not to treat our own children precisely the same way we treat everyone else's. It is my particular obligation to care for my children and to aid their development into mature selves. Though certainly I cannot neglect the demands of justice and ignore the needs of other children, I am required to give a certain preference to my own: if I do not, I am simply refusing to be a father to them. If I try to be a father to everyone, I will only succeed in being a father to no one. Each of us must seek to play the special roles to which we as individuals have been called. This is the only way we can actually love anyone at all, for as finite creatures we cannot serve more than a few effectively.

This understanding—that each of us can in fact serve in love only relatively few persons to whom we are related in our special responsibilities—underlies the Protestant doctrine of vocation. Each is called by God to his particular tasks in society, and there he must work if he would serve the neighbor. No one else can be the father to my children: this is my task. No one else can teach my students that which I have been called to teach them. This is my vocation in God's kingdom, shaped partly by my aptitudes and training, partly by promises I have made, partly by my role as defined by society; if I do not fill it, no one will. God's will that I love and serve my neighbors can be obeyed in this *present moment* only through loving these neighbors whom I confront *here and now in this situation*, and whom I can serve through the particular roles I am here called upon to play. Trying to love everyone equally—as one might suppose abstract justice requires—results in loving no one at all.

It should be clear, then, that the commandment to love involves consideration both of justice and the full range of our various special responsibilities. All demand consideration; none can be ignored. Often, perhaps always, they exist in tension with each other, and we have to forsake some demands to fulfill others. But we can never reduce them to each other, for they are incommensurable. In every situation the demands of each should be weighed against the others before a decision is made. Furthermore, in each new situation there must be a new weighing and a new decision.

These considerations by themselves, then, never tell us the *right* action. It is the act of decision that finally determines what course of action shall be followed in freedom. Thus, we alone are responsible for what we decide, and we cannot avoid bearing that responsibility. However, these considerations do call our attention to requirements of love we might otherwise overlook.

The matters of justice and special responsibilities, however, have not yet brought us to the heart of the Christian conception of love. For the distinctive thing about Christian love is its overriding concern for the sinful. In the parable of the prodigal son, instead of carefully ascertaining that justice be done to both sons—the one punished and the other rewarded—love forgives the sinner and forgets the requirements of justice entirely (Luke 15:11-32). And, to drive home the point, Jesus states explicitly that "there will be more joy in heaven over one sinner who repents than over ninety-nine righteous persons who need no repentance" (Luke 15:7). Obviously, this great concern for the sinful and evil which is at the very heart of redemptive love must seriously qualify what we have said thus far. It is conceivable that in certain situations justice and special responsibilities may have to be disregarded in the name of love for the sinner. For example, though these two considerations seem to require one to defend his family against a murderer, it may be that a Christian ought to have greater concern for the redemption of the murderer than for the safety of his family. Certainly forgetting to love the murderer is not justifiable, simply because of fear for one's family. "If you love those who love you, what credit is that to you? For even sinners love those who love them. . . . But love your enemies, and do good . . . expecting nothing in return . . . and you will be sons of the Most High."

(Luke 6:32, 35.) There is a strong imperative in love toward precisely the one whom we would be inclined to overlook if we took account only of the requirements of justice
and our responsibilities. This third consideration we can
designate, for the sake of brevity, the concern for redemption.

The introduction of this matter does not mean, however,
that the others can be ignored. They also flow from love,
and it is no more justifiable to overlook their demands
than to forget love for the sinner. In every situation we must
weigh each of these three factors against the others in reaching our decision. It is clear they will often be in tension,
pulling us in diverse ways. We are forced inevitably at
such times deliberately to ignore or compromise certain of
the *apparent* obligations laid upon us by love, in the attempt
to do what we have concluded love *really* requires of us.
Obviously, in this kind of complex situation of conflicting
obligations there will be no clear-cut right choice. Nevertheless, we alone must take the responsibility for our
choice, for it will be no one's decision but ours.

There is a fourth consideration that must be brought
into the situation of decision. This is the matter of the distinctively Christian self-knowledge that we are sinners. If
this is indeed self-knowledge—and not merely a dogma
nominally subscribed to—we will know that all of our decisions proceed from our sinful involvement in selfish interests, and that we must, therefore, take special care lest
we convince ourselves we are acting from love when in
fact we are not. Christians will be aware of their tendencies
to delude themselves with rationalizations and will guard
against such. We will know, for example, that in a conflict
between our responsibilities to our families and the require-

ments of justice or concern for the sinner, we often convince ourselves to forget the latter two. Thus a parent selfishly favors his own children, gives them privileges and opportunities, instead of working, for example, for integrated schools and equal opportunities for all children. Again, in a war situation if justice seems to require that we support our nation, we may forget our obligation to love the enemy.

There is not time to multiply examples. The point should be clear. Whenever we are faced with a decision, we will be sorely tempted to take the easier, more self-centered way, and to rationalize away the more difficult claims of love. And this fact, also, must be taken into account in difficult decisions: we must lean over backwards in the direction we would prefer to avoid, in order to allow for our sinful perverseness.

There are, then, at least these four incommensurable matters which must be considered whenever a serious decision is made—all of them required by the imperative that we give ourselves absolutely out of love for our fellows. None can be ignored; none can be reduced to the others. Nor can they be reduced to numerical values and then added up together in the manner of some utilitarian calculus, getting a sum which tells us the "right" thing to do. Every decision requires a kind of intuitive estimate of the claims of each consideration and then a deliberate preferring of one or more to the others. It is the immeasurability and incommensurability of these matters that make every crucial decision what we always know it to be in the hour we are faced with the choice: a kind of stab in the dark or leap into the unknown in which we hope and pray we do the right, but which we always well know may be the wrong.

V

We now have before us in abstract terms the problem which the Christian faces in reaching decisions genuinely responsive to the will of God. In order to make clearer the relevance of this analysis to the actual making of decisions, it is necessary to consider briefly a concrete problem. Almost any significant current issue would be appropriate here—race relations, academic freedom, our agricultural surplus in a hungry world, and so on. However, as the historic peace churches have always understood, the issues for the Christian conscience are perhaps most sharply pointed up by the problem of Christian participation in war. Let us see what light our analysis throws on some of the dimensions of this complex issue.

It should be clear from our discussion thus far that no legalistic solution to this problem can be given for two reasons: First, no legalistic answer prescribing in advance the "right" course of action can be given to any problem faced by the Christian. As we have seen, such would deny the freedom of both God and man and make the relation between them—in this case at least—one of law. And this would violate the very heart of the gospel. Second, the issues in such a complicated question as participation in the defense of one's nation are obviously complex and ambiguous, involving very real tensions between the various considerations we have isolated. Such tensions will be resolved in differing ways by different Christians, the several considerations impressing themselves upon them variously. It is, therefore, not possible to legislate a final "right" answer to the problems involved here. Each Christian must personally bear responsibility before God for his resolution of the issues.

Remembering these qualifications, however, we can briefly try to see what is involved in the question. What light do our four considerations throw on the problem of Christian participation in war?

The implication of the matter of justice, taken simply by itself, is relatively clear. It requires one to align himself with the side, the victory of which, so far as he can tell, will bring more good, or less evil, to more people. Often, of course, it is difficult to make such judgments, but when possible, the demand of justice is obvious.

But complications in this position arise as soon as we remember our third consideration, redemption. Redemptive love is concerned for the sinner. But how does one redeem a sinner through bombing him? How does one reconcile men—so alienated from God and from their fellows as to become aggressors in war—through destroying them? It might still be possible to work redemptively with survivors at the end of a war, but what about those killed? Even if there were an answer to this question, what right has one to kill some in order to redeem others? Though justice—as well as one's special responsibilities to those aggressed against—might seem to require one to fight the aggressor, it is not clear how this can be reconciled with love's demand to work redemptively with sinners. Justice apparently requires us to take sides; redemption seems to question the very possibility of violently opposing aggression.

Further complications enter the picture when one remembers the fourth consideration. If my own nation is at war, clearly my self-interest is involved in her success or failure. In this kind of situation it becomes extraordinarily easy to convince oneself that our side is the just side, we are in the right. The fact that both sides rationalize thus— hardly anyone fighting against his own nation in the conviction that the enemy has the just cause—should qualify one's estimate of the claims of justice in the matter. Is it not likely that the claims of self-interest are the really effective ones here?

Clearly, none of these matters can be assessed certainly and irrevocably. Therefore, it should not surprise us that faithful and honest Christians have disagreed on the proper role for Christians in wartime. Some have concluded it to be their duty to participate in the war effort; others, that they must refuse.

It is necessary at this point to turn to our second consideration, the matter of special responsibilities. In some cases these may conclusively affect the decision. Consider, for example, a Christian who holds the position of secretary of state. When he takes up such a position he takes upon himself the special responsibility to care for the needs of the nation, seeking to preserve it against destruction, and the like. He has responsibilities here by virtue both of the role he is in and the promises he made when taking office. Obviously, as a Christian, he must also be concerned about justice for all men and the redemption of sinners. But when he is working in and through his office, love would seem to require that he give his official commitments priority over these other considerations: to do otherwise would be to break faith with those for whom he has promised to decide and act. And in taking up his office he has agreed to perform precisely this task of making decisions for the nation as a whole.

Clearly the special responsibilities of the secretary of state will require that he seek to avoid war, but it is not clear that he has the right to do so at all costs, e.g., at the cost of slavery, if such is not in accord with the will of the majority of those for whom he must decide. His responsibilities, then, will probably require him to advocate a substantial defense budget, to make defensive alliances against potential aggressors, and the like. The wholesale destructiveness of nuclear warfare certainly complicates these issues enormously, but this problem cannot be discussed here. The important point to note is that most of his *official* decisions will have to be made in the light of his special responsibilities in any case *precisely because those decisions are derivative from and an expression of those responsibilities.* (This in turn implies, of course, that decisions stemming more directly from other roles must in a similar way be appropriate to *them*—here "pacifist" convictions, e.g., might become controlling. However impossible it may be to separate absolutely the various roles played by any one person, they must be clearly distinguished in order to grasp the real moral issues involved in each.) The secretary of state is the man who has been placed by the nation in a position to make decisions for the nation as a whole. If the nation were largely pacifist, it would be irresponsible for him to develop a large defense program. But in a nonpacifist nation—as in twentieth-century America—it would be a failure to fulfill the demands of Christian love upon him, were he to work out a "pacifist" foreign policy. Thus, many of the decisions of a Christian secretary of state will be guided simply by his best judgment on how the responsibilities of his office are to be carried out—though he must make some place also for the claims of justice and redemption.[4]

---

[4] Because of an awareness of these responsibilities of public office, sectarian groups such as the Mennonites have often concluded that a serious Christian cannot participate in government. It is not difficult to see why they have drawn this conclusion. Since a public official must be responsible to all the people—not only to serious Christians—he is unable in his *official* actions to witness very clearly to the radical character of the Christian ethic. Both sectarian thinkers

and those who hold Christians must take responsibility for society have interpreted this fact as the "compromise" which is inevitable when one seeks to apply Christian love to the social order. On the basis of this judgment the former group have called for withdrawal of Christians from responsible positions in society; the latter have regarded "compromise" as a necessary evil.

Both positions are in error. For both have misconstrued as "compromise" the fact that love, in seeking to serve the *other*, must always *relate itself to that other in his actual situation*, whatever be its character. Both, in short, have understood love primarily as *law* (a fixed form of action) rather than as *freedom* (creatively adapting itself to meet the real needs of every situation). When Christian love is understood in terms of Christian freedom, then it becomes clear that the "right" course of action cannot be laid down in any law but must be reached in responsible decision before God. This requires that we take account of love's demand for justice *and* redemption *and* the fulfilling of our special responsibilities. To argue otherwise is to forsake the Christian gospel and the freedom for which Christ has set us free (Gal. 5:1), and to substitute for them a new legalism and thus a new slavery. As Paul rightly says of such legalistic Christians: "You are severed from Christ, you who would be justified by the law; you have fallen away from grace" (5:4).

Far from being compromise, it is precisely the radical demand of the Christian ethic to love without self-concern that may require one to serve his fellows through government position. As Paul reminds us, "there is no [governmental] authority except from God, and those that exist have been instituted by God" (Rom. 13:1). It is by means of government that God orders men in their social relationships. Moreover, in our own time of welfare services, public schools, and the like, there is no question that great and good services are performed through governmental channels, and in certain cases (e.g., in time of economic depression), can only be performed in this way. And this being the case, undoubtedly the special aptitudes, interests, and training of some persons make it their Christian duty before God to enter political life. Moreover, there is no reason in principle why they should not accept such responsible and difficult positions as secretary of state or the presidency. Indeed, *if it is in this role one can most effectively serve his fellow men, it is precisely to this role one is called by Christian love,* however ambiguous and difficult and contrary to one's private convictions may be the decisions required from time to time. God's command is that we love our neighbor regardless of the kind of situation into which this brings

In contrast, now, with the man in a responsible government post, consider the ordinary Christian citizen. Only a very few of his activities, such as voting and paying taxes, involve special responsibilities to the nation as a whole. None of his activities involve such responsibilities in the way the acts of a government official do. *For he is never in the position of being required to make decisions in behalf of the whole nation.* Thus, in his decisions special responsibilities to the nation cannot weigh so heavily as with the government officer. Accordingly, the considerations of justice and redemption will enter with more weight into his deliberations. Perhaps he will find that he must refuse to enter the army when drafted, that, on the contrary, he must publicize the evils of war, seeking to sensitize American consciences in regard to its unchristian character, that he must engage in relief and rehabilitation work, and the like. In short, he may become a conscientious objector.

Whatever be one's views about Christian pacifism in

---

us, not that we squeamishly protect our own moral scruples in order not to dirty our hands. If we really love we must, as Paul put it, even prepare to be "accursed and cut off from Christ for the sake of [our] brethren" (Rom. 9:3), our fellow citizens. We must be willing to decide and act in whatever situation God leads us.

Thus, it is clear that—although nonresistant love is always the appropriate response of Christian individual and group to God's love (and for this reason straightforward nonpacifism as well as "vocational pacifism" must be regarded as inadequate interpretations of the Christian ethic)—because of love's concern for redemption, withdrawal from the evils of society cannot be justified. In the light of Christian freedom, Christian love can be seen as living and plastic in such a way that it both remains nonresistant and yet can take up real responsibilities in the social order.

For a further development of these issues see my article "Nonresistance and Responsibility," in *Concern, A Pamphlet Series for Questions of Christian Renewal*, No. 6, November 1958. (Scottdale: Herald Press.)

general, it is clear that the complex issues here cannot be settled *either pro or con* simply in the abstract. To do so is to neglect what is of central importance for Christian love: the moral demands of the concrete situation in which I am called to decide and act. Right action here as elsewhere cannot be determined by some abstract principle—whether of loyal service in defense of one's nation, or of conscientious objection to all involvement in such activity—but only in conscientious decision in the situation itself. Such decision will always seek not mere consistency with principles, but rather to be responsible to the will of God for that moment, responsive to the radical demands of Christian love in that situation. However, this much at least is clear: no serious Christian may make a decision involving the issues raised by Christian pacifism without giving the most careful consideration to the radical and perhaps undesired responsibilities here laid on the Christian.

VI

We can conclude this brief sketch of the ambiguities and difficulties of the problem of decision by recalling once again the context which gives decision meaning. However careful the deliberation which precedes it, decision as we have noted in this chapter, always involves a leap into the unknown. We may develop guides and principles to help us discern the ramifications of the alternatives confronting us, but the choice itself—the act through which we eliminate certain alternatives with their proper claims and select the one to which we will give ourselves—is entirely our own doing, and we alone must bear responsibility for it. If the only context for our decisions were the confusing welter of claims and counterclaims of our various special responsibilities, of justice, and of redemption, the constant imperative to decide might well lead to despair. But for Christian faith no such result need follow—indeed, the contrary is the case. For within the threefold context we have described, acts of decision have genuine meaning as the real fulfillment of authentic human existence. Consider again the character of this context:

First, the ultimate reality with which men have to do—God—is a genuinely meaningful foundation for establishing the significance of human decisions and actions; for he is apprehended in faith as himself free and creative, loving and forgiving. He has called this world into existence that there might be a community of love and freedom, and he is working out this purpose in the actual course of history.

Second, Christian faith is aware of the concrete actualization of this purpose in a community of genuine love and forgiveness—the church. This community, with its tradition reporting "the mighty acts of God" and its expectation of the coming kingdom of God, provides a haven of purpose and meaning within the otherwise chaotic course of human history.

Third, the Christian knows himself to be called into existence as a free and creative being, redeemed from bondage to the failures and sin of the past in order to realize his freedom within the beloved community. Therefore the leap of decision in freedom and love through which he creatively takes upon himself responsibility for his action is just the moment of his fulfillment, his redemption, his genuine rapport with the purposes of God. It is precisely in the full realization of his freedom that man, as an active and responsible creator, finally becomes what God intended him to be—the image of the Creator himself (Gen. 1:27).

Thus, whereas the imperative to decision might well lead to despair were its only context the social and cultural chaos of relative claims and values, within the context provided by Christian faith, it is just this opportunity to decide, to create, and to bear responsibility for action, that is apprehended as authentic human existence.

> O Lord, our Lord,
>   how majestic is thy name in all the earth!
>
> When I look at thy heavens, the work of thy fingers,
>   the moon and the stars which thou hast established;
> what is man that thou art mindful of him,
>   and the son of man that thou dost care for him?
>
> Yet thou hast made him little less than God,
>   and dost crown him with glory and honor.
> Thou hast given him dominion over the works of
>   thy hands;
>   thou hast put all things under his feet. . . .
>
> O Lord, our Lord,
>   how majestic is thy name in all the earth!
>
>   (Ps. 8:1, 3-6, 9)

Epilogue

I T MIGHT BE THOUGHT THAT THIS ANALYSIS OF THE FREEDOM
and relativity of the Christian ethic implies there is no
proper place for such groups as the Mennonites, who insist
that Christian love must always express itself in radical nonresistance. But this is not so. The Anabaptist founders of the
Mennonite tradition well knew that Christian freedom was
the presupposition of the position they took. This is why
they insisted that church and state must be separate and the
church be a "believers' church." The church can be the
church only when men freely and openly and consciously
decide to respond to God's act of love in Jesus Christ
through loving their fellowmen. But the implication of this
view that both the foundation and the fruition of the Christian community are found in God's calling men in and to
freedom is diversity and variety within the Christian church.
For men in their freedom inevitably understand and respond
to God's call in diverse ways. To expect anything else
would be to suppose God had created a community of
puppets, all cut from the same mold and all acting in the
same ways, not free men. We should not be surprised, then,

to find within the Christian church at large what in fact we do find: a group of subcommunities each clinging to some significant aspect of the gospel which God has enabled them, in their freedom, to see and confess.

The Mennonite church is one such subcommunity. We in this tradition stand here because in our faith we have freely decided this is the position to which God's command has led us, namely, to die martyrs' deaths—if God grant us the strength—before we bear arms against a fellow man. We dare not abandon these convictions, we dare not give up our witness. To do so would be to disobey God's will as we have come to know that will for us. But by the same token, we dare not deny other Christians the right, indeed the duty, to remind us of other facets of the gospel which we may have overlooked and which may contradict our interpretation of God's will. We dare not fail to recognize as Christian brother he who conscientiously and honestly and freely before God concludes that Christian love requires him to participate in the defense of his nation. It may be that because of our differences, he and we cannot witness to the gospel within the same subcommunity in the Christian church. It may be that for the Mennonite community to make its peculiar and essential witness to the rest of the church and the world, it will find necessary the exercise of a discipline which excludes from its immediate fellowship persons of alien conviction. But, as we saw in an earlier chapter, if such action seems required, we should not regard it as more than a pragmatic act, necessary to make a clear witness on this issue which seems to Mennonites central to the Christian faith. No claims beyond that can be made. Indeed, it is essential that every group which knows itself to be the bearer of a unique and perhaps indispensable interpretation of the Christian gospel forthrightly accept in Christian love and fellowship those other subcommunities within the church with which it differs.

God and God's kingdom are more and greater than any of us in our subcommunities within the Christian church can know or imagine. He, after all, is the creator of the heavens and the earth, and we are simply his very limited and sinful creatures. God's revelation is so rich and so full that no human interpretations—or combination of human interpretations—can hold it. It overflows all. Hence, the diversity of views among Christians on theological and moral issues, together with its concrete sociological expression in the variety of subcommunities within the Christian church, is something for which we should be grateful. It is God's way of giving himself to us, not simply in the partiality and incompleteness of our own convictions, however strong and essential they may seem to us to be, but in the wholeness of the faith of the whole church.

There is no call, then, for all denominational groups to forsake the convictions to which they have historically witnessed simply because they have come to realize it is also possible for Christians to witness to contrary convictions. On the contrary, they must forthrightly and openly witness to those convictions which God has granted them—both to church and to world. For only as they make such a witness to the others whom God is also calling, is there justification for their separate existence as distinct communions.

This is not the place to attempt an assessment of the peculiar tasks to which each of the various significant subtraditions within Christendom has been called. If we truly believe in God's providence, it will be clear to us that he has been preserving each for some significant purpose within his church. For the Mennonite community, I would venture to say, that purpose for our day is to become a living witness—in and to the rest of the church—to the demand of love to forsake all defenses of every sort, acting in every sinful and evil situation with real healing and redemption. Were Mennonites to carry out this witness—not in the pride of being the only true Christians but in the humility of being, before God, fellow sinners with the rest—perhaps God would enable them to speak with real effect, and other Christians from other subcommunities within the church would, in their freedom, come also to see this as the will of God for them.

Index of
SCRIPTURE REFERENCES

Index of
PERSONS AND SUBJECTS